WIRED
TO GLOW

WIRED TO GLOW

THE NEW PSYCHOLOGY OF SUPER TRAITS:

WHY NARCISSISTS ARE DRAWN TO YOU AND THE RED FLAGS YOU MISS

CONNIE CROWE, LPC

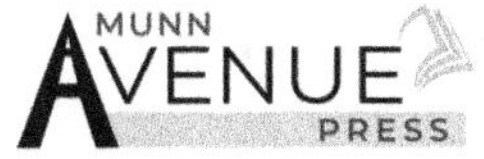

WIRED TO GLOW
The New Psychology of Super Traits:
Why Narcissists are Drawn to You and the Red Flags You Miss

First Edition
Copyright © 2025 by Connie Crowe, LPC

Published by
Munn Avenue Press
300 Main Street, Ste 21
Madison, NJ 07940
MunnAvenuePress.com

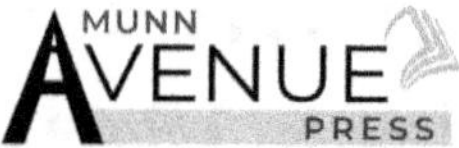

Paperback ISBN: 978-1-960299-99-4
Hardcover ISBN: 979-8-9861680-9-8
Printed in the United States of America

Disclaimer
This book is intended for educational and informational purposes only and is not a substitute for professional mental health care. The author is a licensed professional, but reading this book does not create a therapeutic relationship. If you are experiencing emotional distress or mental health concerns, please seek the support of a qualified therapist or healthcare provider. Everyone's journey is unique, and professional guidance may be necessary to support your individual healing process.

A Note on Names and Privacy
Throughout this book, names and identifying details have been changed, not to protect individuals, but rather to focus on what matters: the patterns, the behaviors, and the impact they leave behind. The stories shared are deeply personal and true to my lived experience. I hope that by sharing what I've lived through, you'll see your own story more clearly and begin to reclaim it.

Contents

Introduction:
The Strength They Hunt

This book is for every strong, successful woman who's ever sat in the wreckage of another toxic relationship thinking, *How did I let this happen again?*

The explanations you've been given haven't held up. And the longer you've tried finding what's wrong with you, the harder it's been to see the actual pattern. I know. I lived it. I'm a licensed professional counselor with a master's degree in mental health counseling. I built a career in behavioral health, served as a corporate executive, and spent years helping others navigate complex relationships. I understood narcissism. I understood personality disorders. And still, I spent four years funding the double life of a man who was soliciting sex from strangers while convincing me we were building a future together.

From the outside, I had it all together. Career, education, insight, boundaries, self-respect. And yet, I fell into the kind of relationship I was trained to spot. That became the turning point. Not when it ended, but when I started digging deeper to understand *why*. And that's what led to the book you are holding in your hands today.

For too long, women have bought into the notion that if you keep attracting toxic men, it must be because something is wrong with you. We're handed a list of traits and diagnoses, such as codependent, love addict, and people-pleaser, and told to fix whatever part of us invited in the dysfunction. The advice sounds logical, but it rarely holds up under real-world scrutiny. Especially when it doesn't explain why we keep finding ourselves in these relationships. We're the ones running companies, leading teams, holding families together, yet we find ourselves in relationships rooted in depletion and control.

Researcher and clinical lecturer in the field of psychopathology, Sandra L. Brown, saw what others missed. In a groundbreaking study with Purdue University, she and her team turned the focus away from the exploiters and toward the women who had loved them: hundreds of survivors who had given everything to relationships that nearly destroyed them. That alone made the research rare. But what she found made it revolutionary: The women most likely targeted by disordered partners weren't broken or emotionally fragile. Quite the opposite, they consistently scored high in two specific traits: agreeableness and conscientiousness. Brown named them Super Traits.

These women are marked by their strength. They are therapists, doctors, lawyers, and business owners, the ones people count on. Women who followed through, kept their word, and made space for other people's needs without abandoning their own, at least before the breakdown began. Women with full lives, stable careers, strong friendships, and reputations for holding it all together.

And that's exactly what predators look for: strengths they can exploit. These Super Traits are the core of what makes you both exceptional and vulnerable:

AGREEABLENESS: THE RELATIONSHIP-INVESTMENT TRAIT

- *Trusting*: You assume the best in others and project your integrity onto them.

- *Straightforward*: Honest, direct, confiding by nature.

- *Altruistic*: Considerate, willing to compromise and sacrifice for others.

- *Cooperative*: Motivated by harmony and mutual support.

- *Modest*: Gentle, self-effacing, approachable.

- *Empathetic*: Tender, kind, forgiving.

- *Loyal*: Committed, even when unsafe.

- *Tolerant*: Open to differing views, slow to abandon others.

CONSCIENTIOUSNESS: THE INTEGRITY-DRIVEN TRAIT

- *Efficient:* Competent, resourceful problem-solver.

- *Organized:* Brings order to others' chaos.

- *Dependable:* Keeps commitments, highly reliable.

- *Achievement-Oriented:* Ambitious, driven, and willing to work through difficulty.

- *Self-Disciplined:* Steady, non-impulsive.

- *Deliberate:* Cautious, careful decision-maker.

- *Values-Driven:* Holds deep personal integrity and strong ethical standards.

These traits are what make you successful at work, in friendships, in life. They're why people trust you, lean on you, and count on you. But low-conscience partners know how to weaponize these strengths. They build a relationship fueled by your generosity, then use your very wiring, your Super Traits, to keep you from walking away.

Psychologists refer to the individuals who operate this way as the Dark Tetrad. Their personality traits include narcissism, psychopathy, Machiavellianism, and sadism. Each trait is clinically distinct, but together they create a behavioral profile defined by exploitation, low empathy, manipulation, and emotional harm. It's estimated that about one in five people possess a high concentration of these traits. And they tend to repeat the same tactics across every relationship they touch.

Here's how those traits tend to show up:

- *Narcissism*: Inflated self-importance, entitlement, and constant need for admiration.

- *Psychopathy*: Lack of empathy or remorse, low consciousness, high impulsivity.

- *Machiavellianism*: Calculated manipulation, deceit, self-serving strategy.

- *Sadism*: Enjoyment of cruelty, escalation of humiliation, calculated harm for sport.

In other words, these aren't random acts of meanness; they're deliberate strategies. Brown's research found that what's strong in the survivor is often missing in the predator. These partners are calculated; they seek out the traits they lack—empathy, stability, and genuine emotional investment. At first, it feels like they're mirroring you, reflecting your best qualities back as proof of connection. But it's not a mirror; it's a siphon. They take those traits to construct a convincing false self, then feed off your energy to keep it alive, slowly draining you in the process.

Most people, including mental health professionals, don't clearly see this. As a result, the harm gets misinterpreted and the survivors get mislabeled. That's because the clinical field still leans too heavily on frameworks that pathologize the victim and overlook the patterns.

When you extend trust, you're called naive.

When you commit deeply, you're accused of being codependent.

When you break down, the assumption is that something was broken to begin with.

But here's what the research actually shows:

- 60% of survivors had no history of trauma.

- Most had stable careers, strong friendships, and healthy self-regard before the relationship.

- The manipulation, gaslighting, and betrayal these women endured created psychological distress where none had existed before.

This is trauma, not temperament. When therapists see symptoms like low self-esteem, confusion, or isolation, they often assume those conditions led to the relationship. In reality, they came from it. Survivors didn't start broken. They were broken down.

When you look closely, the profile is clear: These aren't gluttons for punishment or love addicts. They're driven, capable, emotionally competent women who got caught in the grip of a predator. And they stayed because their wiring made it hard to leave, not because they lacked strength, but because they led with it. This distinction matters because slapping the label of codependency on this does more than miss the mark, it obstructs the path to healing. It strips women of the context they need and leaves them trying to fix parts of themselves that were never broken.

The data doesn't support it. The lived experience doesn't support it. And when we finally stop trying to contort ourselves into the wrong diagnosis, the clarity hits hard. The real recovery begins when we stop pathologizing the women who were targeted and start teaching them how to protect what makes them exceptional.

You'll hear my story, but it mirrors the story of so many others. Another relationship that started with a connection and ended in devastation. Each one had a different shape, but the pattern stayed the same: love, intensity, confusion, betrayal.

Like many women who are competent in every other part of life, I kept wondering why this was the one place I couldn't seem to get right. When I began writing this book, I was already deep in the work of healing. The relationship that nearly broke me had ended, but its impact lingered. I was starting to understand what had happened and how far I'd drifted from myself. What you're holding is the result of that reckoning, not written from the wreckage, but from the hard-won clarity that came after. Once you see the pattern, it's hard to ignore it. And that's where your power begins to return.

You've likely been called names that don't reflect who you are: codependent, wounded, and naive. But if you're anything like me and the women in this research, none of those apply. You're strong, capable, and conscientious. You've been navigating relationships with your whole heart. And now, you're learning how to protect it.

That's what this book is here to do. You'll learn how to recognize the strategies that disordered partners use: love bombing, future faking, mirroring, breadcrumbing, and intermittent reinforcement. You'll learn how and why those tactics are effective, especially for women with Super Traits. You'll see how cognitive dissonance forms, how it scrambles your decision-making, and how to get your clarity back. Most importantly, you'll learn how to reclaim your traits without shame and direct them toward a life that works in your favor.

You're not here to become someone else. You're here to come home to yourself...fully awake, fiercely self-trusting, and equipped to live in a way that honors your depth.

Let's begin.

1

The Attraction Trap: Why Strong Women Fall for Dangerous Men

JOURNAL ENTRY
I'm going to live my best life tonight!
I deserve it!

"Oh my God, look how hot my date is."

The woman at the bar thrust her phone in my face, and she wasn't lying. On her screen was a photo of a devastatingly attractive man. And as I looked up, there he was, materializing over her shoulder with a disarming grin that made him even more appealing in person.

I was drunk on freedom and grief that night, a dangerous cocktail that makes you feel invincible and vulnerable all at once. I'd lost my marriage of ten years, then cared for my mother through her brutal battle with pancreatic cancer, only to lose her too. After that, the country home I'd recently bought to escape the city had flooded, as if the universe was determined to keep me underwater.

I had been the devoted wife, the dutiful daughter, the high-achieving professional. Now, after years of being the responsible one, I was collapsing under the weight of it all. Maybe you know that weight, too. The kind that builds quietly, expectation by expectation, until one day you can't breathe. Some days, I could barely get out of bed. Other days, like tonight, I felt a wild compulsion to declare that I was still alive. On that night, the bourbon blurred the edges between grief and rebellion, loneliness and liberation. Through the dive bar's haze, with my therapist brain switched firmly off, I could be anyone. I could step away from being the woman who'd spent the last few months watching her mother die, or the newly single girlboss trying to hold it all together. I was just another woman at a bar, laughing too loud, living too fast, trying not to be everything to everyone.

Little did I know, in my haste to escape, I was running straight into the arms of danger. Tyler carried himself with an easy confidence that felt authentic rather than arrogant; his country boy charm was disarming. While other guys at the bar seemed desperate for attention, he had the natural magnetism of someone who knew he already commanded it. He was younger than me, but moved through the space like he owned it, somehow managing to hold court while appearing completely unaffected by the attention. It all seemed so effortless, but beneath his casual facade, every detail was carefully curated, from the way his white Henley draped perfectly across his trimmed and toned chest to his artfully tousled dark hair. Needless to say, I was transfixed.

"Are you two together?" I asked, gesturing toward the woman as I took a sip of my drink.

"No," he said, looking at his female friend with a twitch of amusement before turning that smile on me. We started up a conversation about music and his work as a commercial architect. He was intoxicating, funny, and engaging. Unfortunately, I didn't realize then that I was walking into an elaborate game. I was just another potential conquest in Tyler's carefully orchestrated hunt. He'd positioned himself perfectly. The charming facilitator, the non-threatening friend, the attractive stranger who wasn't trying to pick anyone up but somehow had everyone's attention. In that moment, all I felt was the electric current of attraction and the intoxicating possibility of being reckless and impulsive, of living completely in the moment.

The rest of the bar faded away as we fell into easy conversation and playful banter. We inched closer with every laugh, our legs and hands finding excuses to touch. Tyler had this way of making you feel like you were the only person in the room. That's the thing about Dark Tetrad men. They're charming, captivating, and calculated. They know exactly how to shape their story and image to draw in high-value women. He hooked me with stories about his close-knit family and his painful divorce. It all felt real, like someone who'd been hurt but was still brave enough to stay open. Each revelation seemed to be perfectly calibrated to draw me in deeper, though I wouldn't recognize that calculation until much later.

Maybe it was the bourbon. Maybe it was months of pent-up grief and stress demanding release. Or maybe it was Tyler's magnetic pull. But I heard myself say something completely out of character: "Wanna go to the bathroom and make out?"

WHEN THE HUSTLER GETS HUSTLED

Looking back, I realize I was drunk on more than bourbon that night. I was drunk on rebellion against my fragility. I'd left no stone unturned fighting for my marriage and my mother's life. And still, it had all been taken away. But while my life was in full collapse, I was still showing up to work like a boss. Leading a team. Hitting my numbers. Commanding the room. On paper, I looked unshakable. Yet underneath the blazer and lipstick, I was hanging on by a thread.

If you've been there, you know. Crushing it on the outside and quietly unraveling on the inside. When perfection becomes your armor, and your prison. When you've got a calendar full of meetings and a nervous system that never resets.

The bourbon helped, maybe too much. It took the edge off. Gave me something to look forward to. I didn't start as someone who drank to forget. Not at first. But the line moved slowly. A pour here. A heavy night there. I didn't call it anything at the time. I was grieving. I was tired. And so over being strong.

Now, enter Tyler. He's too polished for that bar, too perfect for that night. A wolf in a henhouse. Caught in the pull of his charm, all I saw was the shine, not the darkness I experienced underneath. I prided myself on my ability to read people, my clinical training, and my emotional intelligence. These very qualities became liabilities in the face of his practiced performance.

I realize now that magnetic pull was something more sinister than chemistry. Research shows that individuals with Dark Tetrad personality traits are masters at creating the perfect first impression. They wield appearance and charm like tools, selectively and precisely, all for the one goal, to gain access.

And it works, especially on women like us. The same traits that fuel our success create our vulnerability. Conscientiousness, responsibility, and our drive to maintain control become the very qualities they exploit. We're drawn to their apparent confidence and spontaneity precisely because it offers an escape from our rigid self-control. In my case, Tyler represented everything I thought I needed: Someone who could help me loosen my grip on responsibility, who seemed strong enough to share my burdens, and who made me feel seen in ways my exes never had.

Studies suggest up to one in five men possess these Dark Tetrad traits. In other words, they're everywhere, from boardrooms to bars to dating apps. The charming stranger buying you a drink may be running a well-practiced script. His polished image, disarming humor, and strategic positioning are all part of a calculated performance designed to bypass your natural defenses.

Like Tyler, they present as the perfect package. Educated, career-focused, from a good family. Later, Tyler would show me his architectural drawings, tell me stories about his motocross racing days, and speak about his close relationship with his family. Every detail seemed to confirm he was exactly what he appeared to be. Yet beneath that polished exterior lay something else entirely—someone I sensed could be a predator, but who'd learned how to appear safe.

I am a therapist, trained to recognize manipulation. I'm a career woman and I'm very good at what I do. If I could fall for it, anyone can. And this is why telling this story is so important. These men don't guess who to charm. They calculate it with eerie accuracy, targeting women wired to see the best in others. They know that strong, successful women often carry an equally strong desire to surrender control, if only for a moment. They understand that our capacity for empathy and commitment, usually our greatest strengths, can become our greatest vulnerabilities in the wrong hands.

A PERFECT STORM: THE EMOTIONAL PULL OF DANGEROUS RELATIONSHIPS

The truth is, I saw the red flags and turned them pink. Why? Because I was neck-deep in grief, pressure, responsibility, and the relentless urge to keep performing.

Research shows that Dark Tetrad personality types hunt strong women when they are in situations of emotional vulnerability, such as a recent loss, loneliness, or feelings of overwhelm. They move in during moments when we're still standing but no longer armored. That's when Tyler made his move, using his disclosures to draw out mine.

This is where self-awareness becomes critical. It's not enough to know the warning signs of Dark Tetrad individuals. You need to understand your vulnerabilities to them. When are you most likely to mistake danger for excitement? What circumstances make you willing to ignore your better judgment? For me, it was a perfect storm of grief, stress, and the need to feel something other than responsible. But I've worked with enough women to know countless paths lead to the same destination.

Maybe you're burned out from always being the strong one. Maybe you're tired of so-called nice guys who can't match your intensity. Maybe you're just feeling burned-out from over-functioning in life and work. That doesn't mean you can't have fun or take chances. It means understanding that the very qualities that make someone seem perfect in your lowest moments might be precisely what makes them dangerous.

Dark Tetrad individuals study your longing and shape-shift to match it. The connection feels uncanny because it's crafted that way.

HARDWIRED TO SHINE: THE POWER AND RISK OF SUPER TRAITS

In those early months with Tyler, I blamed myself for not seeing the signs. I was a therapist, after all. I'd spent years studying human behavior, helping others navigate relationships. How could I have missed what now seems so obvious?

The answer came years later through groundbreaking research by Sandra L. Brown at The Institute for Relational Harm Reduction & Public Pathology Education. Her studies revealed what type of traits predators hunt: women like us—successful, empathetic and conscientious. They target our strengths, driven by a desperate need to fill their own void.

In her research, Brown identified two Super Traits that make certain women particularly attractive to Dark Tetrad personalities: high agreeableness and high conscientiousness. These elevated traits, which typically serve us well in life and relationships, become vulnerabilities when paired with someone who lacks them entirely.

Agreeableness manifests as empathy, trust, and an investment in relationships. That night at the bar, my ability to see the best in others, usually an asset, became a liability.

Conscientiousness shows up as loyalty, responsibility, and commitment. The very qualities that made me successful in my career and friendships were the ones Tyler could most easily exploit.

This isn't just my story. Brown's research showed that roughly 60% of women who end up in relationships with Dark Tetrad individuals are successful professionals: attorneys, doctors, executives, and yes, therapists. We're not codependent or love addicted. We're strong women whose greatest strengths become weapons against us in the wrong hands.

Understanding Super Traits revolutionizes how we think about these relationships. Instead of asking "What's wrong with me?" we can recognize that our positive qualities made us targets. This insight gives us language for what we've lived through. And tools to choose differently next time.

For me, this knowledge was vindication. I wasn't weak for falling for Tyler's manipulation. My empathy, conscientiousness, and ability to see the best in others were strengths to protect, not flaws to fix. The key wasn't changing who I was, but learning to recognize those who would use my best qualities against me.

THE DANCE: TWO PATHS FORWARD

I see it over and over in my therapy practice, the same pattern that played out in my own life. We ignore the early signs, convinced our situation is different. "He's working on himself," we say. "He's trying to change." We pour more love, more understanding, more of ourselves into fixing someone who can't be fixed.

Without recognizing these patterns, the dance becomes increasingly dangerous. The manipulations grows bolder, control turns dangerous, and the gaslighting intensifies. Like me, they find themselves tangled in shared assets: houses, cars, businesses. Their world shrinks as they're slowly isolated from friends and family who "just don't understand." By the time they realize what's happening, they're trapped in a maze of financial and emotional manipulation that can take years to escape.

I know because I lived it. Even after losing close to $200,000 while extricating myself from shared assets with Tyler, I was one of the lucky ones. Some spend years trying to co-parent with someone who keeps weaponizing the kids. Some never break free and some face violence when they try.

But there's another path. Understanding your Super Traits, and learning to protect them, changes everything. Imagine walking into a bar or opening a dating app armed with the ability to spot the subtle signs of manipulation. Picture yourself maintaining healthy boundaries not from a place of fear, but from a deep appreciation of your worth.

Envision using your empathy and conscientiousness as the superpowers they are, while staying alert to those who would exploit them.

You can stay open to connection while making sure the right people earn your trust. Your capacity for deep connection and understanding can remain intact. You just learn to reserve it for those worthy of your trust. As a result, the red flags that once looked like excitement start appearing in their true colors. The charm that once seemed irresistible reveals itself as carefully crafted manipulation.

Most importantly, you stop second-guessing yourself. You recognize that your Super Traits aren't weaknesses to overcome. They're strengths to celebrate and protect. The very qualities that made you a target become your greatest defense against those who would exploit them. That's because freedom isn't found in changing who you are. It's found in understanding your worth and refusing to let anyone dim your light.

REAL TALK: HOW TO GUARD YOUR GLOW

Listen, I know you're smart, strong, and capable. Maybe you're running meetings, closing deals, or saving lives by day. And that's exactly why these guys target you. Because you've got the goods they want.

Let me break down what I wish someone had told me over bourbon (or whatever your drink of choice is. These days mine is zero-proof wine, but that's a story for later). Trust those gut feelings, even when they whisper. You know that moment when something feels slightly off, but you think, "I'm being too critical" or "Maybe, I'm overreacting?" That first instinct is your superpower, trying to protect you. Listen to her.

Let me give you the real talk on your Super Traits. Your empathy, conscientiousness, and ability to see potential in others are your superpowers. You just need to be selective about who gets access to them. Your Super Traits don't need fixing. They need protecting. Stay open, but stay sharp. Guard your access. I was about to learn men like Tyler aren't rare, they're everywhere. Masters of disguise and manipulation, seeking to steal the light from women who glow.

 ## LET'S REFLECT

That night I thought, *Wow, he's so open.*

Little did I know I was witnessing a textbook Dark Tetrad strategy: *curated vulnerability.*

That rush of intense attraction? It was a chemical override. My nervous system got tricked.

That's how strong women get hooked.
Pro tip: the bourbon did not help.

Super Traits He Targeted:

- Empathy
- Hopefulness
- Emotional depth
- Responsibility

Red Flags That Looked Like Connection:

- First date confessionals
- Oversharing and disclosure
- Physical intimacy sped up

 # Journal Coaching Moment

Find a quiet space, take a deep breath, and let yourself reflect honestly, without judgment or pressure. This is your space to explore, not to be perfect.

Have you ever felt a crazy strong connection with someone right away?

What did you feel in your body at that moment? Were you excited, safe, anxious, or unsure?

Do you think anyone's ever exploited your best qualities to get close to you? Your caring nature, your hopefulness, your fierce independence?

Looking back, were there any moments early on that felt a little off... but you convinced yourself they were just signs of a deep connection?

2

Spotting Strategic Shape-Shifting

LETTER FROM TYLER
After date one, I was hooked. You are
all the things...smart, funny, witty,
successful, professional, and silly,
creative, affectionate...You make me a
better version of me.

I smoothed my black blazer and checked the mirror one last time before walking into a neighborhood sports bar where the cheap beer and wings matched my modest expectations. Two days had passed since our bourbon-fueled bathroom makeout session, a wild, reckless night where nothing existed but the moment. Tonight was supposed to be different: a proper first date, albeit a casual one.

I'd chosen my outfit strategically: professional but sexy, the polished executive who could still turn heads. My armor, really, a reminder that I was still the composed, successful woman I'd worked so hard to become, even if my personal life felt like it was held together by safety pins and prayers.

The familiar wall of noise hit me as I walked in. TVs blaring from every angle, the clash of voices rising to meet them, the constant motion of servers weaving between packed tables carrying towers of wings and buckets stuffed with domestic beer. I scanned the crowd, looking for the sharp-dressed hottie who'd held my attention at the bar on Saturday night. Instead, I found an overgrown adolescent hunched over the bar, already nursing his second drink, wearing a wrinkled gray hoodie that looked like it had been pulled from the bottom of a laundry basket.

It wasn't until he turned and flashed that same disarming grin that I was sure it was him. "Hey...you," he said, clearly struggling to remember my name. "Wow, you look... really nice."

I slid onto the barstool next to him, now hyper-aware of my blazer, the low-cut silk top underneath, and the effort I'd put into looking effortlessly put-together. "Thanks," I said. "You look... comfortable." I laughed, still trying to reconcile these two versions of the same man.

The contrast was jarring. Saturday night, when he was prowling for a hookup, he'd been meticulously pieced together. But now, on an actual date where we might explore the potential for something real, he couldn't be bothered to grab anything more presentable than a hoodie.

Still, chemistry has a way of ignoring dress codes and soon we were in deep conversation. His casual admission about forgetting my name turned into playful banter, and I found myself relaxing despite my initial surprise at his appearance. After the weight that settled over the final years of my marriage, the lighthearted humor was exactly what I needed.

The attraction from Saturday night hadn't faded either. If anything, it was stronger in the clarity of relative sobriety. Tyler matched my energy effortlessly, as if we've known each other for years. His laugh was infectious, his wit quick, and the way he leaned in slightly when I spoke made everything feel intimate despite the blaring TVs and shouting sports fans surrounding us. Every time I mentioned something about myself—my knack for solving problems, my unapologetic love for 90's alternative music, my passion for helping others—he'd light up with recognition, sharing a similar passion or value. The night flowed with an ease that made my plans for a responsible early night seem suddenly rigid and unnecessary.

Almost as if reading my thoughts, Tyler's eyes narrowed. "You know," he said, his voice low enough that I had to lean in too, "I need to check on my puppy at the office. He's a Doberman, just a few months old. The office is right around the corner...wanna meet him?"

The invitation hung in the air between us, its true meaning crystal clear despite its innocent packaging.

I raised an eyebrow. "You brought your puppy *to work*?"

"Can't exactly leave him in my apartment all day," he said with a sly grin that promised trouble worth having.

I knew I should call an Uber and head home. I had meetings in the morning, responsibilities, and a carefully ordered life I was trying to rebuild. But the lure of a puppy and Tyler's casual confidence in his invitation made all those sensible concerns feel trivial.

"A puppy, huh?" I smiled, already reaching for my purse. "That's a pretty good line."

"Is it working?"

His eyes followed mine as I stood from my seat and grabbed the jacket I'd draped on the stool. I told myself I was reclaiming my freedom, embracing spontaneity after years of rigid control. My body hummed with whiskey and anticipation as his hand found the small of my back, guiding me toward the exit. The lingering scent of his cologne and the promise in his smile overwhelmed any last whisper of caution.

I didn't realize I was walking straight into a carefully laid trap, one baited with exactly the right combination of danger and safety to draw me in. All my training as a therapist, all my pride in reading people and situations, evaporated over bourbon and banter. I didn't stop to ask why we were clicking so intensely, so fast. Why someone so polished could also feel disheveled and raw. Why that duality pulled at me like a magnet. I couldn't put my finger on it. Have you ever been so drawn to someone's charm that it made you blur right past the parts that didn't add up? Looking back, I probably should've known better than to follow a stranger to a second location in the middle of the night.

I didn't care. I should have. But by then, I could already taste him on my lips.

WHEN SUPER TRAITS BECOME SUPER LIABILITIES

The red flags from that night seem painfully obvious as I lay them out in writing. Most telling was the stark contrast in Tyler's presentation. Two nights earlier at the bar, he'd been meticulously groomed and dressed like he modeled for *GQ*. Now, for what was ostensibly a chance to explore a real connection, he couldn't be bothered to wear a clean shirt. That shift should have made me pause, not as proof of something sinister, but as a signal to pay closer attention to what else might not align.

At the time, though, all I saw was possibility. It's a common trap for women like us: seeing potential where we should be seeing patterns. But this kind of disparity isn't a coincidence. Evolutionary psychologists argue that Dark Tetrad traits may have developed as part of a "cheater strategy" in mating, designed to exploit short-term opportunities while dismissing the value of genuine commitment.

This same strategy was evident in his choice of venue. On its own, the loud sports bar might've seemed like a casual, convenient choice. But add in his intensity and the rushed intimacy, it felt more like a setup. A tactical move designed to amplify chemistry and keep things surface-level. The blaring TVs and packed crowd forced physical proximity, making meaningful conversation nearly impossible. We had to lean in close to hear each other, our shoulders touching, the chaos around us making our connection feel more intense than it was. Like his carefully disheveled appearance, the environment was orchestrated to maximize short-term attraction while avoiding the kind of genuine dialogue that might lead to something real.

His head start on drinking was another warning sign I rationalized away by thinking, "he's allowed to have a drink or two to unwind." Sure, we'd had our uninhibited moment Saturday night, but this time was different: He was already several drinks in before I arrived. I later discovered through research that overdrinking can be a common trait among individuals with Dark Tetrad individuals, a manifestation of their poor impulse control and constant craving for stimulation. Yet in that moment, it just seemed like a continuation of our weekend spontaneity.

Perhaps the most insidious warning sign was his perfect mirroring of my values and interests. Each time I shared something personal, whether about my career goals, ethical values, or personal interests, he'd immediately claim to share the same perspective. Dark Tetrad individuals are masters at this kind of mimicry, especially when there's potential for gain. They understand that appearing to share our values and traits builds trust quickly, particularly with those of us who possess the genuine versions of these qualities.

But here's what makes these early encounters so treacherous: Each red flag played perfectly into the specific traits that usually serve us well. My straightforwardness had me misreading his red flags as virtues. As a result, forgetting my name became charming honesty, his sloppy appearance a sign of authenticity. My natural cooperativeness had me following his lead rather than questioning why he chose a setting where real conversation was impossible. Most dangerously, my high tolerance for discrepant behaviors had me explaining away the dramatic change in appearance instead of recognizing it for what it was: what I later perceived as a fundamental devaluation of our date.

This is how Dark Tetrad individuals operate: They manipulate our emotions by targeting the very traits that fuel our success elsewhere. They understand that women with our traits will question our skepticism before questioning their motives, work to maintain harmony even when something feels off, and take responsibility for making interactions work smoothly. They see an opportunity to use our positive qualities against us.

READING THROUGH THE CHARM

But our Super Traits don't need to be a dating liability. By understanding how Dark Tetrad individuals target and exploit these traits in early interactions, we can protect ourselves while maintaining the authenticity and empathy that make us who we are.

In healthy environments, our empathy, trust, responsibility, and loyalty make us remarkable friends, leaders, and professionals. These same traits become vulnerabilities only when exposed to manipulation. They're why people depend on us. They're why we excel. And with the right awareness, they can also become our strongest defense.

Let's break down that first date with Tyler to see exactly how this works.

IMPRESSION MANAGEMENT

What Happened: Tyler dramatically changed his presentation from our first meeting to our first date, from polished and put together to deliberately casual and unkempt.

What I Think It Means: Dark Tetrad individuals are masters of impression management. Research shows they invest significantly more time in their appearance than average, but strategically vary it to achieve different effects. The polished version attracts initial attention; the casual version creates an illusion of authenticity and vulnerability.

The Protection: Note dramatic shifts in presentation. While everyone has different sides, rapid and strategic personality shifts early on often indicate impression management rather than genuine complexity. A green flag is a person who is consistent in appearance and behavior.

STRATEGIC VULNERABILITY

What Happened: Tyler turned forgetting my name into a moment of disarming charm, making a potential faux pas seem endearing.

What I Think It Means: Dark Tetrad individuals excel at what researchers call Strategic Vulnerability: showing just enough apparent weakness to seem human and relatable, without ever truly letting their guard down.

The Protection: Pay attention to the timing and impact of seemingly vulnerable moments. Are they genuinely revealing something meaningful, or merely designed to make you feel overly comfortable or disarmed? *Always* check your gut in these moments.

ENVIRONMENTAL CONTROL

What Happened: Tyler chose a loud sports bar where meaningful conversation would be difficult, forcing physical proximity and making emotional connection seem more intense than it was.

What I Think It Means: Dark Tetrad individuals often control early encounters to maximize chemistry while minimizing genuine getting-to-know-you conversation. The noise, the need to lean in close, the brushing of my hair behind my ear, the casual atmosphere all serve to create artificial intimacy.

The Protection: Suggest meeting somewhere that allows for actual conversation. Someone interested in genuinely knowing you will welcome this. Someone focused on manipulation will usually resist or redirect. Manipulators will always tell you who they are. When they do, walk away.

CONTROLLING THE PACE

What Happened: Tyler suggested checking on his puppy at the office, an innocent-sounding excuse to escalate physical intimacy.

What I Think It Means: Dark Tetrad individuals excel at controlling the pace of interaction while making it seem like natural flow. They create situations where you feel like you're freely choosing, while they're actually directing every move.

The Protection: Notice who's controlling the pace and direction of interactions. And watch out, ladies, the puppy routine will get you every time! No matter how exciting the proposition might seem, a genuine connection doesn't require overriding your boundaries or better judgment.

This framework allows us to maintain our Super Traits while protecting ourselves from those who would exploit these qualities. The goal isn't to become less trusting or empathetic, but to become more discerning about who deserves our trust and empathy.

This can't be stressed enough: Your Super Traits aren't weaknesses to be corrected, but strengths to be protected. Just as Wonder Woman had to learn to control her powers rather than suppress them, we need to learn to wield our Super Traits skillfully rather than let them be used against us.

Research supports this approach. Studies show that women who understand how their Super Traits can be exploited are significantly more likely to spot manipulation early, while maintaining healthy relationships in other areas of their lives. They don't become less empathetic or understanding; they simply become better at recognizing who deserves these gifts.

Paranoia isn't the outcome. Clarity is. Real intimacy develops at a pace that feels comfortable for both parties. Real vulnerability is reciprocal, not strategic. And real chemistry doesn't need to bypass your boundaries to prove itself.

THE DOWNSIDE OF SEEING THE BEST IN OTHERS

Without recognizing these early patterns, the intimacy dance becomes increasingly dangerous. I watched it unfold with Tyler. What started as an innocent-seeming appearance shift evolved into constant shape-shifting. To me it seemed that the man who showed up disheveled to appear more authentic on our first date later also appeared to craft different personas for different audiences: the talented architect at family gatherings, the life of the party with his friends, and the devoted boyfriend on social media.

The strategic vulnerability that seemed so charming that first night, like forgetting my name and laughing it off, turned out to be more than a fluke. As the relationship unfolded, I started to notice a pattern: Whenever something felt off, another moment of vulnerability would appear to smooth it over. It wasn't always clear whether it was calculated or just convenient, but it kept me emotionally invested when I should've been paying closer attention to my escape plan.

As time went on, Tyler's environmental control expanded beyond loud bars. He'd choose restaurants where he knew the staff, positioning himself as the charming regular. He'd suggest group activities where I'd be slightly out of my element, seemingly to cultivate dependence on his guidance. Every setting seemed to be carefully chosen to keep me off balance and maintain his advantage.

And the pace control that began with a puppy visit accelerated into a whirlwind. Within months we were planning to move in together. Within a year, we had joint assets that would later cost me thousands to untangle. Each escalation felt like my choice in the moment, but looking back, I can see how masterfully he orchestrated every step.

But there's another way this dance could've gone. Imagine recognizing that first strategic appearance shift, noting how someone switches personas, and asking yourself why. Picture maintaining a comfortable distance when someone deploys strategic vulnerability and observing whether their actions match their emotional displays. Envision suggesting alternative meeting places when someone tries to control the environment, watching their reaction when you assert your preferences. How do they respond?

Most importantly, imagine trusting your initial instincts about pacing. When someone suggests checking on their puppy at midnight, you don't have to question whether you're being too rigid or untrusting. You can simply say, "That sounds cute. I'd love to meet him over coffee tomorrow instead." It's a way to control the pace and see how he responds when things aren't tilted in his favor.

The goal isn't to shut yourself off from risk or adventure. It's to learn how to spot when spontaneity is being used as a smokescreen. Someone who respects you will respect your boundaries rather than looking for ways around them. A man who's genuinely interested in knowing you will be happy to meet where conversation is possible. The man who's truly vulnerable with you won't weaponize that vulnerability to escape accountability. And the man who actually wants to build something real with you won't rush to entangle your assets before you've had time to see his true character.

REAL TALK: SEEING THROUGH THE CHARM

I know first dates are complicated enough without having to scrutinize every little thing. And when chemistry's crackling and the booze is flowing, the last thing you want to do is overthink it. But here's what I wish someone had told me that night at the sports bar: A single red flag, like a dramatic shift in presentation, might not mean much on its own. But for those of us with Super Traits, it should be a cue to proceed with caution. That perfectly polished player from Saturday transformed into Monday's casual, vulnerable guy to test which version gets the best response. Paired with other signs, it can be a clue that you're dealing with someone who is carefully crafting their image to fit the situation.

In my case, the red flags kept flying, and I kept shooting them down. But if I could intercept old me as she stepped away to pee and ponder, this is what I'd say:

Pay attention to shifts in presentation, but also take note of the environment. If a potential partner chooses a loud bar where real conversation is impossible, it's worth asking yourself why. Suggest meeting somewhere quieter next time. A man genuinely interested in knowing you will welcome the chance to remove the hindrances to real connection. A man focused on manipulation, on the other hand, will want to keep you close and off-balance, relying on distractions to control the narrative.

Notice who's controlling the pace. Is he always the one suggesting the next move, the next location, the next drink? Take back the wheel. Make a suggestion of your own and see how he handles not being in control.

Most importantly, trust those first instincts. In that moment when something feels slightly off but you start rationalizing, that's your intuition sending up a flare. Don't silence it with "Maybe I'm being too harsh" or "I should give him a chance." Trust your gut. Your intuition is your second brain, processing what your heart hasn't caught up to yet.

Here's the bottom line: That first meeting and that first real date set the tone for everything that follows. You know how to read people and situations in your professional life. Now it's time to bring that same discernment to your dating life. No more second-guessing your instincts. No more letting charm override your common sense. If he's already showing you multiple versions of himself, controlling your environment, and pushing the pace, it's not going to get better. It's going to get worse. Knowing all this now doesn't mean I knew it then.

Of course I should have gone home. The smart choice, the self-respecting choice, was to thank him for the drink, call that Uber, and leave with my sense of self intact. My openness, my trust, my willingness to see the best in others weren't flaws to fix, but gifts to safeguard. They weren't meant to be handed over to someone who hadn't earned the right to hold them with care. True connection requires more than a rush of whiskey-fueled impulsiveness. It takes time, respect, and reciprocity. But at that moment, knowledge was no match for chemistry. The heat, the thrill, the strange relief of feeling seen; I was clinging to the rush, hoping it would lead somewhere safe. So, when Tyler held the door open and we stepped into the night, all those rational voices in my head faded into a seductive haze of what-ifs. My heart raced with the pull of temptation. I told myself it was just a fling. A little freedom, a little fun, a little moment to forget.

But deep down, I knew better. I was about to cross a line I couldn't uncross and follow a path that would blur the edges of pleasure and power, connection, and control.

And the truth? The danger made it all the more irresistible.

 ## Let's Reflect

That night, I told myself, *This feels so real.*

What felt so real was actually engineered intimacy, manufactured to deceive.

That thrilling pace, the rush of it all?

It wasn't destiny. It was *deliberate acceleration*, disguised as romantic spontaneity.

And I fell for it because I'm wired for connection. Not because I was naive.

Because I lead with my heart. Because my Super Traits, when unguarded, became access points.

Super Traits He Exploited:

- Optimism

- Courage to connect quickly

- Desire for mutual depth

Red Flags That Felt Like Romance:

- Personal disclosure

- Intense chemistry

 ## Journal Coaching Moment

Find a quiet space, take a deep breath, and let yourself reflect honestly, without judgment or pressure. This is your space to explore, not to be perfect.

Have you ever looked back at a relationship that felt deep and instant only to realize later it was too much, too fast? What details stand out now?

Can you name a moment when someone's perceived vulnerability made you feel special, but in hindsight, may have been used to manipulate trust?

Which of your best traits are you most proud of? And how can you protect them without dimming them?

3

Chemistry and Control: How Dark Tetrad Men Accelerate Intimacy

The best sex I ever had was with a true psychopath.

He looked like Jakob Dylan in that "One Headlight" video. If you don't know who I'm referring to, welcome to your 90's rock education. The son of Bob Dylan had brown hair, piercing blue eyes, and a James Dean swagger that made everyone want to either be him or sleep with him in 1996.

As if that wasn't enough, this guy hit the genetic lottery for talent. He was a gifted artist and soccer star. He introduced me to The Pixies and Sonic Youth, music that felt dangerous and raw. It was the sound of pure rebellion that perfectly matched our chaotic connection. Of course, I didn't realize then that this beautiful disaster was checking every box of the psychopathy checklist.

Our electric encounters were raw and primal, pushing boundaries I didn't know existed. His touch lit up every nerve ending, leaving me breathless and desperate for more. The intensity was addictive. Everything felt heightened, explosive, like we were writing our own rules for how we perceived love should feel.

But here's the thing about beautiful disasters: They always leave wreckage in their wake. The same intensity that made our connection so intoxicating eventually turned toxic. His jealousy evolved from possessive to paranoid. Those piercing blue eyes that once made me weak in the knees began to flash with unpredictable rage. The fights that used to end in passionate reconciliation started ending with shattered glasses and bruised hands. He'd apologize with the same conviction he'd shown talking about art or music, making promises that felt real until they weren't again.

Yet every time, I convinced myself it would be different. That the passion was worth the pain. Until the night he wrapped his hands around my throat, and I saw nothing but cold emptiness in those beautiful eyes. I was too young and too inexperienced to recognize the red flags staring me down.

I probably should have learned my lesson then, but I chalked it up to the naivety of youth. As I followed Tyler through that deserted industrial office park, that vaguely familiar rush of danger felt like the promise of release. I was self-aware, successful, and a decade wiser, too smart to fall into old patterns.

And after months of being the responsible one, holding everything together through loss and chaos, didn't I deserve a little fun?

Tyler's Dobermann, Duke, a solid fifty pounds of muscle, nearly knocked me down as we walked through the office door, sending us both into a fit of laughter that echoed off the concrete walls. We cracked beers from the break room mini fridge while he gave me the tour, but we both knew where this was heading. The sexual tension was electric, building with every step as he led me through the darkened hallways.

It was that familiar magnetic pull, that skin-on-fire chemistry that overwhelmed me the moment Tyler lifted me onto his desk. The easy strength in that impassioned display of dominance and lust left me breathless, my body responding before my brain could object. His hands in my hair, his mouth on my neck, and suddenly nothing else mattered. Not the meetings I had tomorrow, not the professional image I tried to maintain, not my carefully constructed boundaries.

But we soon realized that office sex is never as sexy as it looks in the movies. We knocked over a cup of pens, sent papers flying, and I nearly concussed myself on a filing cabinet when he tried to get creative with positions, killing ourselves laughing at how badly we'd botched the whole sexy office fantasy.

Even through the awkwardness, the intensity transcended the physical. "I've never felt like this before," Tyler whispered between kisses, his voice hushed with what seemed like genuine emotion. Feeling wanted and hearing those words lit up something primal in me. At forty-something, newly divorced, and unsure of my place in the dating world, his focused attention and evident desire made me feel sexy and alive in a way I'd forgotten was possible.

The magnetism between us was undeniable, like gravity pulling two planets into orbit. His touch, his scent, the way his eyes followed me across a room. It all awakened parts of me I thought had gone dormant during those final years of my marriage. When he looked at me like that, all my anxieties about dating in my forties melted away. I was no longer some middle-aged divorcée trying to figure out modern dating. I was instead desirable, magnetic, and powerful.

All the while, I reminded myself this was just a fling. I wasn't that starry-eyed girl anymore, mistaking intensity for intimacy. And after losing my marriage and my mother in the same year, I was reclaiming my freedom, one reckless night at a time. And this one was the cherry on top.

But as Tyler's hands traced the outline of my hips down to my thighs, I couldn't help remembering how my first relationship had ended, the casual cruelty behind the passion, the way he could flip from tender to terrifying in an instant. I dismissed those warning signals and surrendered to the physical sensation, the chemical rush of skin on skin. What were the odds of this happening again?

• •

As I slid into that Uber at 3 a.m., my body humming with satisfaction, a familiar thought flickered at the edges of my mind: *Why does this feel so good and so familiar?* I felt alive, electric, like I was waking up after a long sleep.

In truth, I was drawn to a fire I'd danced with before. Yes, I was strong, successful, and self-aware. But here I was again, tangled up in a thrill that burned hot and fast, the same kind I'd watched turn to ash more than once before.

Though I didn't realize it at the time, cycles like these repeat themselves until we recognize and break them. However, by the time your traits are being exploited, the groundwork has already been laid. The charm, the chemistry, the early intimacy. That's when the red flags start to blur, and dangerous behavior begins to feel magnetic. Even familiar.

But on that night, I brushed away all of the warning signs. After all, I kept telling myself, this wasn't going anywhere. But deep down, the girl who dreamed of more still held onto hope. Maybe it could lead to something meaningful and beautiful.

THE CHEMISTRY OF TOXIC ATTRACTION

The brain in love looks an awful lot like the brain on cocaine. Do you know that intense attraction you feel with someone new? It lights up the same reward centers that make addictive substances so dangerous. Your amygdala processes the thrill and danger, while your reward and satisfaction centers create intense cravings for more contact. Together, they override your usual good judgment, making even the most grounded woman mistake chemistry for compatibility.

Dark Tetrad personalities know this in their core, and they're experts at triggering that addictive response. They follow a calculated recipe, perfected over time: intense eye contact that floods us with feel-good chemicals; hot-and-cold behavior, also known as emotional tug-of-war, where one person withdraws and the other is drawn in. Together, they keep us craving more and mirroring our deepest desires until it feels like fate. This carefully orchestrated cycle, known as intermittent reinforcement, hooks us deeply. They leverage this rush of chemicals like skilled con artists, fooling even the smartest women into thinking they've found the real deal.

That's the part that wrecks you most. You think it's rare, sacred, real. But to him, you're one in a long line of targets. I know this stings. It did for me, too!

The Dark Tetrad individual might feel the thrill of the chase and the excitement of conquest, but they can't form the real bond you're feeling. It's like two people dancing to completely different songs. You're swaying to a love ballad while he's moving to the primal beat of the chase.

Authentic connection grows slowly, like a fire you carefully feed. But Dark Tetrad types are all about the explosion, creating something that feels like destiny but leaves you burned. And they're not just performing. In the moment, they do feel the intensity. They are predators, after all.

But because of their need for constant stimulation, intimacy is fleeting, a rush that blurs fantasy and reality. When the moment fades, so do they. Therefore, they can walk away without a scratch, leaving you to sift through the ashes of something that felt so real, yet was never real to them.

For successful women, this creates a perfect trap. Their emotional intelligence and high empathy, usually their secret weapons in relationships and careers, become a liability. They're exceptional at reading people, attuned to the tiniest shifts in tone or expression. However, when a Dark Tetrad man's intensity feels genuine in the moment, it is. But here's the trap: You're feeling the thrill of connection while he's feeling the thrill of the hunt. These opposing objectives create a dangerous illusion, leading women to mistake this flash of intensity for true compatibility, thus seeing sincerity in what is really just their own capacity for intimacy reflected back at them, which is also known as mirroring.

Driven women want to excel, which only deepens the trap. Used to solving every problem they face, they tackle relationship red flags with the same determination that made them successful. When things feel off, they don't back away. They try harder. They are sure that they can crack this puzzle like they've cracked every other challenge. But by the time reality cuts through the chemical haze, they're in deep, wondering how their usually spot-on judgment led them so far off course.

These situations don't unfold because you're naive or desperate. They happen because some men are exceptionally skilled at spotting and exploiting the very qualities that make you valuable, your emotional intelligence, your need to understand, and your instinct to nurture potential. The same traits that make you a powerhouse in your career and your healthy friendships can leave you vulnerable to the kind of emotional fraud that men like Tyler have been honing their whole lives.

THE POWER OF PACING

Imagine walking into a first date completely confident in your boundaries, not rigid or closed off. Your empathy and warmth still shine, but they are grounded in understanding your worth. When he suggests moving things to a more "private location," you smile and say, "I'm enjoying getting to know you. Let's save that for when we know each other better." And instead of second-guessing yourself, you feel powerful.

It was no coincidence that the intense attraction I felt with Tyler flashed me back to the transcendent sexual rush I'd felt with my first psychopath years ago. Evolutionary psychologists have uncovered something fascinating about Dark Tetrad individuals; their traits often create an almost irresistible sexual charisma. When you add in the chemical cocktail our bodies produce during passionate sexual encounters, such as oxytocin, dopamine, lowered cortisol, and heightened serotonin, it's like mainlining pure bliss. Every touch feels meaningful, every moment seems destined, convincing you you've found something profound.

These are some of the most powerful biological impulses that drive human experience, which is precisely why our *own* evolutionary adaptations are so precious. Our capacity for patience and our instinct for discernment aren't arbitrary or old-fashioned. They're sophisticated survival mechanisms, honed over millennia.

Women with Super Traits possess deep loyalty and high tolerance for ambiguity, differing opinions, and inconsistent behavior, making us naturally inclined to stay the course and offer second chances where others might walk away. We see potential in others and have the hard wiring to let things unfold organically. We're willing to invest time in building something real. In this way, we're built to forge lasting bonds and build sustainable partnerships.

The problem, then, isn't our natural inclination toward tolerance and loyalty. Rather, it's the immense worth of these traits that makes men like Tyler so eager to claim them. The problem is when we let someone else's urgency override our intuition. Think about it: In every other area of your life, you recognize that anything worth having is worth waiting for. You didn't rush through med school or fast-track your way to that executive position. You understood that mastery takes time and commitment. Why should intimate relationships be any different?

I'm not saying we should never act on attraction or that every intense connection is toxic. I'm saying that when you feel that overwhelming pull, that's exactly when you need to slow down. Not because you're afraid of passion, but because you respect and trust yourself enough to let it unfold naturally. Instead, picture yourself in that moment of intensity, fully aware of the chemicals flooding your system, and choosing to ride that wave without letting it crash you into the rocks. Imagine feeling all that passion, that magnetic pull, and still maintaining your boundaries. Not from a place of fear, but from a place of self-worth.

Because here's the truth: The very qualities that make you vulnerable to the manipulation of toxic partners also make you magnetic to men with genuine intentions. So, what's the difference? Good men will respect these traits rather than exploit them.

The right person will still be there tomorrow. The next day. The next week. Real chemistry doesn't expire. It ripens.

REAL TALK: RIDING THE CHEMICAL WAVE

I know that feeling. That earth-shattering, can't-think-straight, everything-feels-destined kind of chemistry. Trust me, I've been there, and more than once. And I'm not here to tell you to never act on it. I'm here to help you navigate it with your power intact.

Here's your practical toolkit for when that chemical rush hits:

- **Build in breathing room.** No, literally. When you feel that magnetic pull, take a physical step back. Go to the bathroom. Get some air. Give your brain a chance to cut through the chemical haze. Those feel-good hormones are real, and they're powerful. They're also temporary.

- **Set your pace before you need it**. Have your boundaries ready to roll, like muscle memory. "I have an early meeting" is your best friend. "Let's save something to look forward to" is another good one. Seriously, practice these in the mirror, because the time to figure out your lines isn't when you're already swimming in oxytocin.

- **Pay attention to pressure.** If he's great with your boundaries at first but starts pushing harder, that's information. A man who respects you will match your pace, not try to accelerate it. Write that down. Tattoo it somewhere if you have to.

- **Trust those flashbacks.** If something feels familiar in a way that makes your stomach tighten, even if you can't put your finger on why, listen to that feeling. Your body remembers patterns your conscious mind might want to ignore. It's not just déjà vu. Your body is most likely trying to protect you.

- **Keep your squad close.** Text your best friend before your date and have someone who knows where you are. Not because you're in danger, but because having that connection to your real life helps keep you grounded when the chemistry starts clouding your judgment.

- **Play the movie forward.** When you're feeling that overwhelming pull, pause and imagine yourself the next morning. The next week. The next month. Are you still feeling powerful? Still in control of your own story? Still proud of your choices?

- **Give yourself a two-drink maximum.** Alcohol lowers inhibitions and can make it harder for your rational brain to override primal instincts. Personally, I've started telling dates upfront that I don't drink on the first date. It's been surprisingly revealing. Some men respect it, while others self-select out. Either way, their response tells you everything you need to know about their true intentions.

Most importantly? Remember this: Your capacity for deep connection, your ability to see the best in others and your willingness to invest in something real aren't weaknesses to overcome. They're superpowers to protect. And just like any superhero, you get to decide when and how to use them.

The rush isn't going anywhere. The chemistry won't expire. A man worth your time will still be there tomorrow, still magnetic, still interested. But now with the added attraction of someone who respects your boundaries.

Make no mistake: Your compassion, independence, and faith in others are strengths. But have you ever noticed someone using these as a doorway in, only to later use them against you?

Because here's the hard truth: People like Tyler don't stumble into our lives. They *study* women like us.

They know what makes us glow, *and* what makes us give.

So, reflect on this:

- Are you confusing connection with intensity?

- Are you racing toward someone who's mirroring your dreams... or manipulating them?

Next time your body lights up with attraction, ask yourself:

- Is this chemistry... or a chemical trap?

You can ride the wave *without* letting it carry you away.

Here's the bottom line:

That first surge of chemistry isn't random. That's the MO of Dark Tetrad men: orchestrating and fast-tracking connection. And the quicker they can get you hooked, chemically, emotionally, physically, the less likely you are to walk away when things start to feel off.

That's because they know that once you're bonded, once that

oxytocin has blurred your red flag radar, you'll begin to rationalize and minimize their threat. Instead, you'll reach for the memory of who they were at the beginning, the charming, attentive version, and convince yourself that's who they really are, and everything else is temporary.

When you're wired the way we are for loyalty, empathy, and seeing potential, it's a reflex to hold on to that version. To believe in who they could be, instead of who they're showing us now.

That's why your pacing, your discernment, and your boundaries matter so much. The rush will still be there tomorrow. So will the right man. That's because true connection respects your pace, and real love never asks you to override your instincts.

Because here's what I finally learned: True power isn't in how fast you can move. It's in knowing you can stand still in your worth and let others rise to meet you there.

Now go forth like the badass you are, boundaries firm and lie detector fully charged.

 **LET'S REFLECT**

That night, I thought, *"This feels like fate."*

But what I was caught in was chemical confusion, dopamine disguised as destiny. What felt like euphoric clarity was actually my biology being hijacked.

That's how strong, smart women fall for the *wrong* kind of spark.

Super Traits He Targeted:

- Emotional intelligence

- Deep empathy

- High tolerance for ambiguity

Red Flags That Looked Like Intimacy:

- Intense physical chemistry on night one

- Oversharing framed as "deep connection"

 ## JOURNAL COACHING MOMENT

Find a quiet space, take a deep breath, and let yourself reflect honestly, without judgment or pressure. This is your space to explore, not to be perfect.

Have you ever had a moment with someone that felt electric, like you were *meant* to meet?

What did your body feel at that moment? Was it exhilaration, safety, butterflies, or something harder to define? Think back: Was there a part of you that questioned the pace, even slightly?

Did you quiet that voice in the name of "openness" or "chemistry"?

4

Dangerous Devotion: From Love Bombing to Strategic Vulnerability

FROM TYLER

I've never been able to be this open with anyone. You're not like the others—you actually get me. You're different. You're confident, not crazy like my exes.

"My God, he's the perfect BF!"

I texted those words to my friend as I watched Tyler, shirtless in jeans, playing with his Dobermann puppy in my backyard. In just a few short weeks, he'd seamlessly woven himself into the fabric of my life. The house that had felt so empty after my mother's death was now filled with his laughter and the warmth of his constant presence. Even his cheap cologne, a scent I'd normally wrinkle my nose at, now felt like home.

Every morning with Tyler began the same way: A sweet note with his favorite line, "*I cherish you. Can't wait to see you tonight, Beautiful.*" But it didn't stop there. He even remembered the tiniest details of our conversations, surprising me with little gestures that showed he was really listening. For example, the first time I told him I craved pizza on my period, he took note. From then on, like clockwork, period pizza and flowers arrived each month. After years of feeling unheard in my marriage, here was a man who seemed to anticipate my needs before I could even express them.

But it was the pineapple earrings that truly did me in. I'd told him about my mom's pineapple plant, how she'd spent two years nurturing it from the crown of a store-bought fruit, and she always sent me proud progress updates and silly photos. How cutting into that homegrown pineapple on a golden Sunday afternoon had been one of our last happy memories together before pancreatic cancer ravaged her body. And how, every time I saw a pineapple, I thought of her unconditional love, her infinite patience, her ability to nurture life from the smallest seed of possibility. Well, a few days after telling him this, Tyler handed me a small velvet box. I didn't expect much, some little gesture, maybe a thoughtful trinket. But when I lifted the lid, my eyes welled up. It wasn't just jewelry. It was proof that he had been listening and that he *truly* cared. The pineapple earrings were delicate, simple, and probably cost less than dinner out. And yet, I wouldn't have traded them for anything. They represented everything I was desperate to believe: That someone was really listening, really seeing me, and really understanding the depth of what I'd lost.

"Just because," he'd said with that disarming smile. "I know how much she meant to you." In that moment, I melted. But now, looking back on that moment, I feel a gut punch. It was diabolical.

I traced the silver outline with trembling fingers, fighting back tears. After months of people awkwardly avoiding the subject of my mom, or worse, offering empty platitudes about "better places" and "time heals all wounds," Tyler's gesture struck a chord so deep it brought tears to my eyes. The gesture felt like a supernatural sign, like my mom was somehow reaching through him to remind me I was still loved, still seen, still worthy of the kind of nurturing attention she'd always given so freely. Here, finally, was someone whose attentiveness made me feel, for the first time in a long while, that I wasn't navigating my grief alone. Someone who would notice the little things, remember the important stories, and anticipate my emotional needs the way she had.

I thought I was falling in love. But what I was really drawn to was the version of myself he reflected back at me. He'd become the perfect mirror, amplifying my glow, masking his shadow. Within weeks, he was taking work calls from my house. He started including me in family conference calls to discuss holiday plans, as if we'd known each other for years. For someone who had just lost their foundation, his eagerness to include me felt like something steady to hold onto.

So, when he suggested being exclusive, ditching our respective rosters to focus on building something real, it seemed like the natural next step. We had so much in common, such explosive chemistry, such an instant sense of rightness. Not to mention, he confessed he thought he'd never love again until he met me.

And yet, there were small moments that made me pause, moments I couldn't quite ignore. The way his tone sharpened ever so slightly when other men showed interest in me. He called it being "protective." The way he used my given name in love notes. Constance. Only my mother had ever called me that. Sheepish apologies for minor text indiscretions with female "friends." It all seemed plausible and innocent.

And as our worlds merged, Tyler began sharing more about his past. He'd been married twice before. He was young and impulsive the first time. To him, because of his religious faith, marriage equaled sex; he said with a smirk, "And I wanted to have lots of it." Tyler's second marriage had ended when he started causally seeing another woman, but he justified it by saying his wife had already filed for separation and cleaned out their shared apartment. He even showed me evidence to prove she had only married him for a green card. But in me, Tyler claimed to have found something different. I wasn't "crazy" like his exes. I was mature, successful, and grounded. We had what he called "hippie love," the kind of pure acceptance he'd never experienced before.

I couldn't help but notice, at the center of every story was Tyler, the innocent victim, the good guy who kept getting burned despite his best intentions. But once again, I sped past every red flag. After all, wasn't this the story of Beauty taming the Beast, of Anastasia Steele healing Christian Grey? Wasn't this what a whirlwind romance was *supposed* to feel like? Intense. Finally feeling heard. Lives intertwining fast?

I wanted to believe I'd finally found the man who wouldn't just stand by me, but truly see me. I wanted to believe that the pineapple earrings were the prelude to a happy life together. Besides, Tyler seemed so receptive when I voiced my concerns. He'd open up about his traumatic past, sharing stories of his strict upbringing, the pressure he felt to keep racing motocross through injuries, and the abandonment he'd endured in previous relationships. Vulnerability like that couldn't be fake. Could it?

I wanted it to be real. And so I allowed myself to fall deeper, turning red flags into pink, and trusting that those uneasy flickers in my gut were nothing more than ghosts of past hurts trying to steal this present moment of happiness. Our story would be different. We would heal together. Love would prevail.

THE RIPPLE EFFECT

I feel so stupid to have fallen for this. I thought I was impervious to manipulation due to my built-in therapist bullshit detector. And yet, all the while, the teacher was getting schooled! The pineapple earrings were a masterclass in psychological manipulation.

Tyler calibrated every element perfectly: the timing, when grief had left me most vulnerable; the symbolism, transforming my loss into connection; the presentation, casual yet meaningful, "Oh, just because." But this wasn't conscious genius—it was the instinctive wiring of a disordered man who knew exactly how to exploit pain. Through this single gesture, he positioned himself as the one person who truly understood my grief, who could fill the void my mother's death had carved.

This is what psychologists call the Idealization Stage. It's performance, not partnership. And it feels magical because it's meant to. Narcissistic and manipulative individuals mirror your values, hopes, and dreams to lock you in, not to know you. You think you're falling in love. But what you're really doing is falling for the script.

One of the most potent weapons in the idealization phase is love bombing, an overwhelming flood of attention, affection, and gestures designed to sweep you off your feet. The daily good morning texts. The surprise flowers at work. The thoughtful gifts that prove he remembers every detail of your conversations. The constant stream of compliments about how special, how different, how perfect you are.

Those are all examples of love bombs.

Equally calculated was Tyler's sharing of his past. Each revelation served to create deeper intimacy. His strict religious upbringing, the pressure to keep racing motocross through injuries, and his previous marriages all painted Tyler as someone who had been hurt but wanted to open up, and had cast me as the one uniquely capable of understanding his pain.

Through Strategic Vulnerability, Dark Tetrad individuals encourage their targets to reciprocate, creating a false sense of mutual understanding. These tactics seem obvious in hindsight, but research explains why they work so well. We're wired to value what we carry ourselves. When we see warmth, reciprocity, and openness, we lean in and offer the same. And that's exactly what they're counting on.

Research shows these low-conscience types are remarkably good at appearing genuine and trustworthy, especially to women with heightened emotional responsiveness. Your deep capacity for loyalty and commitment builds lasting, meaningful relationships. In the wrong hands, these same traits become the reason you stay long after you should leave. The Dark Tetrad's narcissism, Machiavellianism, sadism, and other low-conscience traits all revolve around the same core playbook: manipulation, emotional detachment, and calculated control.

Again, the idealization stage is all about performance, not partnership. And it feels magical because it's meant to. Narcissistic and manipulative individuals mirror your values, hopes, and dreams to lock you in, not to know you. You think you're falling in love. But what you're really falling for are the love bombs into submission before you even know you're under attack.

The rise of online dating has made this dynamic even more dangerous. Dark Tetrad individuals can now craft multiple perfect personas simultaneously, testing different approaches and refining their manipulation techniques through trial and error. The controlled environment of dating apps allows them to carefully manage their self-presentation, revealing only what serves their purpose while concealing red flags behind carefully curated profiles and calculated disclosures.

When Tyler showed up with those earrings, maybe my therapist brain should've clocked the pace and intensity of such an offering. When he cried over his exes, always playing the one who'd been betrayed, I wish I'd asked myself why he was unloading so much, so fast. Instead, my empathy interpreted these gestures as emotional depth. My conscientiousness appreciated the apparent thought and effort. My agreeableness dismissed warning signs as mere cynicism.

This, again, is the cruel paradox at the heart of these tactics. Yes, these are our strengths, but to someone practiced in deception, they are a roadmap to our blind spots. And what makes these early relationship tactics so effective is how they work in tandem. Love bombing overwhelms you with attention and affection, while strategic vulnerability creates an illusion of emotional intimacy. All along, Tyler was manufacturing trust by positioning himself as wounded but willing to risk vulnerability with me because I was worthy.

Dark Tetrad individuals expertly combine these approaches, using our natural empathy and emotional intelligence against us. They craft a perfect storm of intensity and intimacy that makes their targets feel uniquely chosen, understood, and capable of healing their carefully curated wounds. But it's a trap, the kind that whispers, *If I love him enough, maybe he'll finally feel safe. He's not like the others. He's just misunderstood.*

THE POWER OF PATTERN RECOGNITION

A single silver pineapple earring sits in my jewelry box. I came across it the other day while cleaning, and it struck me how perfectly that pair seemed to represent everything I wanted to believe about Tyler and our connection. The other earring is lost now. Fitting, really, given how the whole illusion eventually fell apart.

That's the thing about understanding patterns: once you see them, you can't unsee them. Like a Magic Eye picture suddenly snapping into focus, all the disconnected pieces form a clear image. Those earrings zeroed in on my deepest wound to bypass my defenses and deepen my trust. In retrospect, the timing was almost surgical, waiting until I'd shared enough about my mother for him to understand exactly how to position himself as the one person who truly "got it."

Tyler was clever enough to know that I would respond favorably, even though every perceived spontaneous gesture, every seemingly genuine disclosure, was a game. When Tyler shared sob stories, he wasn't letting me in. What he was doing was testing my capacity for empathy and gauging how I respond to manipulations. When he mirrored my interests so perfectly, from music taste to design aesthetics, he wasn't discovering delightful coincidences. No, Tyler was crafting a persona designed to make me feel bonded to him. Someone else might have thought his country boy demeanor was put on a little thick. But they tugged my Super Traits, and as a result, felt so disarmingly genuine. At the time, these imperfections only made him more endearing, reinforcing the belief that I'd found someone real in a world of social media polish and corporate pretense.

Research shows that Dark Tetrad individuals follow remarkably consistent playbooks in relationships. They've learned, through trial and error, exactly how to exploit the emotional intelligence and empathy that make their targets successful in every other area of life. But here's the beautiful irony: the same pattern recognition that makes us vulnerable becomes our sharpest weapon once we know what we're looking at. That's because the very traits they tried to exploit—our empathy, our intuition, our depth—become the shield. And with that clarity comes strength. We stop handing our Super Traits to people who haven't earned the right to hold them.

Think about it: Dark Tetrad individuals succeed because they know exactly what they're looking for, women with the emotional depth they lack, the genuine empathy they can only mimic, and the capacity for connection they'll never truly feel. They study our fears, our soft spots, calibrating their performance to slip past our defenses unnoticed. And this pattern doesn't exist only in intimate relationships. I've seen the same dynamic unfold in boardrooms and offices, dressed up in power suits and corporate jargon. What gets sold as radical candor or fearless feedback often lands more like precision-engineered belittling designed to keep people flustered, striving, and second-guessing. Those offhand comments, public critiques, and quiet power moves? All performances. Like method actors, they mirror, manipulate, and position themselves for control.

But what happens when we start studying them back? When we understand that their strategic vulnerability isn't intimacy but infiltration? Knowledge becomes power. Not the kind that hardens us or makes us cynical, but the kind that lets us maintain our depth while protecting our boundaries. Remember this: You don't have to stop being empathetic to stop being exploited. You just have to get better at recognizing the difference between strategic vulnerability and the real thing.

My emotional intelligence, pattern recognition, and ability to see beneath surface behaviors had made me successful professionally. Once I understood what I was really seeing, these same qualities became my strongest defense. Just like I could spot a client's defense mechanisms or recognize therapeutic resistance, I could learn to identify love bombing for what it was: a tactical maneuver rather than a genuine expression of feeling. Our capacity for real connection remains intact when we understand these patterns. We just become more discerning about who deserves our trust.

Those pineapple earrings taught me something invaluable. Yes, they proved Tyler was paying attention. But not to honor my grief or deepen our connection. He was studying me to learn exactly how to position himself as the perfect boyfriend and to groom me to look past future transgressions and boundary-breaking. But now I know real gold doesn't need to sparkle to prove its worth. It simply endures, authentic and unchanging, no matter what light you shine on it. Sometimes the most valuable things we gain from loss are the lessons that light our way forward.

That's the real power of pattern recognition. Not in changing who we are, but in understanding how to protect what makes us special. Once we learn to recognize their playbook, the very qualities they try to use against us become our strongest defense.

The single earring in my jewelry box reminds me now not of what I lost, but of what I gained: the ability to see clearly without losing my capacity to feel deeply.

THE CULT OF PERSONALITY

"He cooked me good meals, gave me lots of kisses, and made me feel good and wanted. He wanted to go everywhere with me. Other than the food, the rest of it completely ceased later."

These reflections could have been pulled straight from my journal, but they're not mine. These are the words of Canadian actress and podcaster Sarah Edmonson, describing her introduction to NXIVM, what she believed was a self-improvement organization that turned out to be one of the most notorious cults of our time.

The parallel is impossible to ignore. As a therapist, I know a thing or two about cult dynamics. However, seeing these survivors' stories laid bare alongside my own experience with Tyler creates an unsettling translucency. Love bombing, strategic vulnerability, and perfectly calibrated attention to emotional needs are the tools Tyler used to draw me in. And they're the same one cult leaders like Keith Raniere groom devoted followers.

"I was at a low point in my life, and they gave me hope and a sense of direction," another NXIVM survivor recalled. God, that rings familiar. When Tyler found me, I was drowning in grief and uncertainty. Like Raniere, he didn't settle for comfort. He became the solution to every unspoken ache, the one person who seemed to truly understand. Men like Tyler create a cult of two, an alternate reality where they are the source of all emotional sustenance. Just as Raniere convinced his followers to share their deepest secrets, which he later used as leverage, Tyler pushed for profound intimacy almost immediately. Each vulnerability I shared was met with seemingly perfect understanding, each confession with apparent reciprocal openness.

Do you still think it couldn't happen to you? NXIVM attracted doctors, lawyers, actresses, and entrepreneurs, women who probably thought the same thing. Just like I did, despite being a trained therapist who understood manipulation tactics. The Dark Tetrads don't prey on the obviously vulnerable. They specialize in making brilliant, capable women doubt their own intuition, until we can no longer trust what's real and what's illusion. Which brings me back to that survivor's haunting recollection: "Other than the food, the rest of it completely ceased later." Even the most polished act starts to crack with time. Whether it's a cult leader's mask of benevolence, a partner's facade of perfect attunement, or a coworker's strategic charm, the truth eventually emerges. Performances like these require constant energy and attention, and once they believe they've secured the person, or sense that the illusion is slipping, they no longer bother to maintain it.

Psychologist Dr. Ramani Durvasula puts it simply: Narcissistic individuals "cannot keep the mask on for long." Studies confirm that the idealization phase often unravels within weeks or months, exposing the manipulator's true patterns once the initial grooming phase has served its purpose. And these dynamics play out far beyond cults and headlines. They happen in everyday relationships when performance is used to exploit belief, empathy, and hope.

How many successful women had to watch their lives unravel before the truth of NXIVM was finally revealed? How many months did I spend trying to reconcile Tyler's early perfection with the manipulator he revealed himself to be? But the question isn't whether the performance will end. It's how much of ourselves will we sacrifice before we recognize it for what it is?

REAL TALK: WHEN THE ROMANCE FEELS TOO PERFECT

Not every whirlwind romance is a love story. Sometimes, it's a carefully laid trap. The sooner you spot it, the sooner you can protect yourself.

You know that feeling when everything seems almost too perfect? When he's hitting every note just right, anticipating your needs before you even express them? Yeah, that's exactly when you need to slow your roll and pay attention. This is when we need real depth perception. That's because real romance can be hard to spot when it's wrapped in well-rehearsed tactics. The more we understand the difference, the better we protect what makes us powerful.

First, let's talk timing. A thoughtful gesture six months in, when someone really knows you? Beautiful. A deeply personal gift just three weeks in? Could be romantic, could be research. Just make sure you're the one writing the story, and not the subject of someone else's scheme.

Watch how they handle your boundaries around disclosure, too. You'll notice a pattern here if you take a step back and look objectively. Here's the thing: There's nothing wrong with vetting your prospects. If you say, "I'm not ready to talk about that yet," and they respect it, green flag. If they push for deep intimacy immediately while making you feel guilty for having walls, red flag. That's because they're not trying to get to know you, no matter how much you would like them to. They're gathering ammunition instead and making you feel uncomfortable with your boundaries.

And don't forget, this starts long before you ever meet in person. We already know that men high in Dark Tetrad traits curate their online personas to manipulate. They tailor their profiles, conversations, and even their vulnerabilities to make you feel like you've met your perfect match. So, if a guy seems uncannily in tune with your tastes, your dreams, your pain, ask yourself: Did he find a kindred spirit, or did he just find your Instagram page?

Make sure to pay special attention to the vulnerability they're putting out there. Are they sharing real, processing-in-the-moment stuff? Or are these perfectly packaged stories about how they've been wronged, complete with convenient morals about how different you are from everyone who hurt them? Take it from me, who learned the hard way: Truly vulnerable people sometimes stumble over their words. They don't have their pain cataloged and ready for presentation.

Here's a quick gut check: Does every romantic gesture feel like it's designed to make you feel chosen and special? Or does it feel like it's genuinely about you? Tyler knew exactly when to give me those pineapple earrings. Not because he cared about my grief, but because he'd studied exactly how to position himself as my savior.

And please, watch for this one: If they're telling you how they've never felt this way before, how you're different from all the rest, how fate brought you together... while simultaneously pushing to accelerate intimacy? That's not destiny. That's a scam. You're getting love bombed.

THE TICKING CLOCK ON FALSE INTIMACY

Dark Tetrad individuals don't build intimacy, they simulate it. But simulation has a shelf life. When Tyler leaned in close with misty eyes and said, "I've never been able to be this open with anyone," I thought I was witnessing vulnerability.

But I wasn't. I was witnessing expiration. These individuals rely on emotional fast-tracking because they can't maintain consistency. So, they borrow your language, mirror your emotional intelligence, and ride the momentum of their love bombing until their nervous system can't hold the weight of sustained connection. That's because Dark Tetrads can imitate love, but they can't live in it. They can't fake emotional depth for long because they don't *have* it; this is a byproduct of their pathology. And that's when the idealization collapses. And what fills its place? Confusion. Self-doubt. The slow erosion of trust. Not because you changed, but because their act hit its limit.

I know what you're thinking: *But sometimes it really is that magical!* And you're right: *sometimes* it is. So, what's the difference? Real connection builds gradually. Real intimacy develops naturally. Real vulnerability is reciprocal, not strategic. So, when in doubt, slow things down. Slow. Things. Down. If he's the right one, he won't mind. Someone who's love bombing will either amp up the pressure or start to lose interest when their tactics don't work.

Remember: You're not paranoid for protecting your heart. You're not a prude for pacing intimacy. And you're definitely not broken for having boundaries. You're just getting smarter about who gets access to that beautiful, empathetic soul of yours. Because here's what I know now: When someone's truly falling for you, they're not plotting the perfect way to prove it. They're probably a little nervous, a little messy, a little real. They're not trying to sweep you off your feet. They're trying to walk beside you instead.

Keep your heart open. Keep believing in love. Just make sure the romance you're being served isn't too perfectly plated. Because a real connection doesn't need staging. It just needs authentic presence and time to grow and to feel safe. Trust me on this one. I've got the lone pineapple earring to prove it.

 ## LET'S REFLECT

That night, I thought he was being real and vulnerable. But what I was really witnessing was the mask beginning to slip.

What I thought was deepening intimacy was actually the unraveling of a performance. A performance designed to hook me. Fast. Because Dark Tetrads know they can't sustain this act.

That spark? That high? It was chemically induced confusion. That's how women with strong boundaries get bypassed, by design.

Super Traits He Targeted:

- High trust in people

- Belief in second chances

- Tendency to self-reflect instead of suspect

- Emotional availability

Red Flags That Looked Like Emotional Progress:

- Early apologies laced with trauma stories

- Tearful "I've never told anyone this" moments

 ## Journal Coaching Moment

Find a quiet space, take a deep breath, and let yourself reflect honestly, without judgment or pressure. This is your space to explore, not to be perfect.

Think back. Have you ever dated someone who came on strong, then suddenly seemed to fade or shift?

Did they say all the right things early on, but over time, their actions didn't line up?

What changed first, your feelings or their behavior?

5

From Matching Pajamas to Mosh Pits: When Chaos Starts to Creep Into the Fantasy

LETTER FROM TYLER
Sometimes I really do feel like I have two personalities.

Three months earlier, I was sitting in a jail cell.

The cold concrete bench. The harsh fluorescent lights. My mugshot face was vacant, drained, and with eyes wide with fear. A DUI at forty-two years old.

I had been unraveling for months, but this? This was the moment everything caught up with me.

My mother died in May. My divorce was nearly final. I had moved to a new town, started a new job, and was grasping at anything that might make me feel in control. Instead, I was spiraling. I was drinking too much, saying yes to things I should have said no to, and numbing myself in every way I could.

That night in September wasn't supposed to end in handcuffs. I went out for birthday dinner and drinks. Two Jack and Cokes, nothing outrageous. I felt fine. Responsible, even. I left my car behind, went back to a friend's house, slept for a few hours, and woke up feeling clear-headed. I thought I was good enough to drive.

Turns out I wasn't.

Somewhere on the quiet, early-morning stretch of highway, flashing blue lights filled my rearview mirror. I wasn't speeding, wasn't swerving, wasn't doing anything suspicious. But it was late, and I guess that was enough of a reason to pull me over.

When the officer asked if I'd been drinking earlier, I told the truth. A few drinks earlier in the night, but I had slept for hours. I had my wits about me. But when I blew into the breathalyzer, the number flashed just over the legal limit: 0.09% Enough to make me a criminal.

I barely remember the officer reading me my rights. What I do remember is the humiliation of sitting in that holding cell, hands trembling as the weight of it all came crashing down. This was more than a bad decision. It was a flashing neon sign that I was losing control.

In the months that followed, I tried to pick up the pieces. A weekend in jail, probation, mandatory breathalyzer screenings, DUI classes. I had no choice but to get my life together, at least on paper. But emotionally, I was still drowning. By the time Christmas came, I was running on fumes. I needed an anchor, something that could hold me together.

That's just what Tyler's family gave me. A Hallmark Christmas, wrapped up with a bow.

Christmas movies. Homemade hot chocolate. Matching pajamas and traditions that felt effortlessly wholesome. His mom bustled around the kitchen, humming along to Christian Christmas music on Alexa. His dad made polite conversation with me over coffee, easing into small talk that felt like the early steps of getting to know each other. His sisters curled up on the couch, sipping wine, scrolling their phones, and exchanging inside jokes. It was familiar, the kind of Christmas I had once taken for granted. My mother had made our holidays feel like magic, like home. I couldn't bring myself to face Christmas without her, or my aunt and uncle, my second set of parents, who had died within days of her.

So, at a time when being alone felt unbearable, Tyler's family opened their arms and pulled me in. His mother welcomed me like I was already a part of them. His sisters included me in their teasing and holiday banter. Tyler was affectionate, pulling me close under the brightness of the Christmas tree, rubbing my back like second nature as we all sat around opening gifts.

But even then, there were moments. Tiny things, easy to explain away.

The way Tyler spoke to his mom. Short, clipped, and flat with indifference. The way his dad was distant, watching from the sidelines rather than engaging. His sisters' occasional side glances at each other when he spoke, like they knew something I didn't. Tyler was the golden boy. That much was clear. His mother doted, his father tolerated, and his sisters...well, they seemed to have their own unspoken understanding of who he really was.

But I surrendered to the moment and chose not to read into it. Every family has its share of unspoken tensions, complicated parent-child dynamics, and inside jokes that don't always feel like jokes. Nobody's family is perfect. So nothing I saw registered as a red flag. It was all just the normal push and pull of people who had been living in the same patterns for decades.

And compared to where I had been three months earlier? This was safe. This was warm. This was *home*.

••

New Year's was supposed to be a reset. It's my favorite holiday, the one time each year I plan something adventurous, a chance to wipe the slate clean and set my intention for the coming year. But this trip carried more weight than usual. I needed renewal. Stability. A sense of normal. And inviting Tyler was my way of folding him into the life I was trying to rebuild.

We went to New York. Along with his ex, Kim. On the surface, it seemed like an odd mix. But surprisingly? I liked her. Kim wasn't at all the type of woman I'd expect Tyler to date. I also never got the sense that anything was still going on between them. She had long since settled into the good friend category, and I genuinely enjoyed her company. Then there was Tye, Tyler's friend from New Jersey. The four of us rented a tiny Airbnb, met up with Tye's friends in the city, and fell into a pattern of sightseeing, bar hopping, and day drinking.

A lot of drinking.

Too much drinking.

By the second night, Tyler's alcohol intake had taken a turn. I felt he was becoming sloppy and combative. The kind of drunk where you watch someone shift from charismatic to dark. He disappeared for hours at one point, then reappeared out of nowhere, grinning like nothing had happened.

And then came the mosh pit. Suddenly, it was 1994 again. It was not in a club. Not at a concert. It was in the middle of our tiny Airbnb. Tyler, deep in a drunken spiral, decided that Kim, Tye, and I needed a demonstration of what it felt like to be in a mosh pit. I didn't need the lesson as I'd been opening up the pit since I was fifteen. But that didn't matter. Tyler was in performance mode. At first, it was stupid, ridiculous. There was shoving and laughter. But then, his hands were on me, and not in a playful way. Overpowering. He was uber strong.

He knocked me down hard, again and again. That's when the laughing stopped, at least for me.

For the first time, I felt it. Not only the embarrassment, though I felt that too, but the heat rising in my face as I tried to laugh it off in front of people I had just met. But it was more than that. I was stunned and afraid. The kind of fear that makes your stomach drop. The kind that tells you, in a split second, you're not safe. And then, just as suddenly, Tyler let go of me. Smirked. And acted like it was all a game. I went along with it. I swallowed the unease, told myself it was nothing, and focused on the holiday ahead.

By New Year's Eve, we were all worn out, and honestly, I was fine with that. A bar, a few drinks, some people I barely knew. It felt easier to keep things light than sit with what had happened. I assumed the best. I told myself Tyler was letting loose after the holiday time with his family.

And that's exactly what I believed.

Until Vegas.

And Jamaica.

And the time he jumped out of my moving car.

But we'll get to all of that.

THE FIRST CRACK

I woke up on New Year's Day hungover, drained, and uneasy. But I told myself it had just been a weird trip.

The drinking should have been my first clue. Here I was, still untangling the legal mess my DUI had created, fresh off confronting my own relationship with alcohol, and suddenly I was immersed in what felt like a four-day bender. But Tyler took it to another level entirely. While the rest of us were buzzed and social, he seemed to be chasing oblivion, drinking until his eyes went dead, his personality flatlined.

Research suggests this wasn't random. Men with Dark Tetrad traits are wired for addiction as their brains are constantly hunting for the next dopamine hit, whether it comes from alcohol, drugs, sex, or chaos. This is classic high-sensation seeking behavior. Or what some would call adrenaline junkies, people who are always chasing something to feel alive, even if it destroys everything around them. My first boyfriend had been the same way. He used whatever substance was available to chase that edge.

I now found myself sliding into familiar roles: the babysitter, the damage control, and the one trying to keep things from completely going off the rails. My friends call me "the mama bear" for a reason: I step up when other people fall apart. And here I was again. Three months after my DUI, I was back in the cycle. While I was not drinking destructively myself, I was enabling someone else's spiral. Trading one form of chaos for another.

Yes, Tyler had gotten sloppy and unpredictable. Yes, he had gotten aggressive. Yes, I had watched something in him shift. His face blank, his eyes vacant, like there was nothing behind them at all. But I didn't leave. I didn't even fully let myself acknowledge how wrong it had felt. Instead, I excused it.

But I couldn't deny that the mosh pit felt like more than a drunken misstep. It was the first real crack in the mask, the moment something was revealed that didn't match the man I thought I knew. But acknowledging that meant facing an impossible contradiction: How could the same person who held me close on Christmas morning suddenly feel dangerous? How could someone switch so completely from warm to cold, from gentle to threatening?

This mental whiplash is what researchers call Cognitive Dissonance. And it is what keeps so many of us stuck. When facts conflict with the feelings forged in those early months, our brains scramble to make sense of it. We question our perception rather than the Dark Tetrad's character. Sandra L. Brown calls it "being both Jekyll and Hyde." It's a level of personality instability that goes far beyond emotional ups and downs. And that instability becomes disorienting. The constant shifting between personas leaves you emotionally seasick as you swing between love and disgust, trust and suspicion, until you lose your own internal compass.

The man who had made me feel safer than I had in months suddenly felt dangerous. The one who excited me more than anyone had in years now exhausted me. The profound connection I thought we shared had revealed itself as something sinister, a void where empathy should be.

Even the company he kept felt wrong. At forty-something, I found myself crashing in a tiny Airbnb with people a decade younger, living like I was in my thirties again. My values, my standards, everything that anchored me was getting murky. But instead of trusting that discomfort, I questioned myself. Was I being too rigid? Too judgmental?

That's how it starts. Not with obvious red flags, but with subtle shifts that make you doubt your reality. The rules shift. The values you lived by start to blur. Things you never would have tolerated slowly become your new normal.

But at the time, I didn't see it that way. Tyler wasn't always bad.

Sometimes he was sweet. Sometimes he was fun. Sometimes he was the guy who held me and called me beautiful and made me feel like I had finally found someone who was committed. So, I let it go.

And that's what I kept doing. I minimized, explained away, and convinced myself that his worst moments were just that, moments. It would have to get worse. More erratic. More humiliating. More painful. It would have to become impossible to ignore and undeniable even to me.

And it would.

THE POWER OF RECOGNITION: UNDERSTANDING COGNITIVE DISSONANCE

After years of therapy and coaching, the truth finally hit me. My emotional intelligence, my faith in human goodness, my instinct to smooth things over, all the traits that made me professionally successful, were the same ones that kept me paralyzed in destructive relationships.

When you have high agreeableness like I do, seeing for the best in people is your default. So, when Tyler showed me warmth at Christmas, it fit perfectly with the way I wanted to see him. When he turned cold and frightening in New York, it cracked that picture wide open. But my mind did what so many of us do when we hit that kind of rupture: We reach for the version that feels safer. The one that lets us stay.

Maybe you've done it too. Told yourself a story that made someone's worst moment feel like a fluke instead of a warning. That's the trap. It feels like protection, but it's really distortion. Psychologists call this **Selective Exposure**. It's like your brain has a bouncer at the door, only letting in evidence that supports what you want to be true. For example, the thought that Tyler is loving and attentive gets a VIP pass.

But the thought that Tyler just physically intimidated me gets turned away at the door.

That's how cognitive dissonance works. Your brain will do backflips to maintain its preferred reality. And if you have Super Traits like mine? Those backflips become Olympic-level gymnastics. That's because when you're built on integrity, on follow-through, and on doing the right thing even when it's hard, your system can't handle the whiplash of emotional inconsistency. Hot one day, cold the next. Nope. Your brain kicks into overdrive, trying to make it make sense, because if it doesn't, then everything you believe about trust and character starts to feel unstable. And that's not something you can sit with for long. It goes against everything you believe about how people should behave and how relationships should work.

Looking back, what really got to me wasn't the heavy drinking itself. It was watching my values erode in real time. The woman who was becoming sober-curious, who had sworn to maintain better boundaries, was suddenly making excuses for someone else's drunken spiral. That contradiction created confusion for me.

Sandra L. Brown, who studies these types of relationships, explains that women with Super Traits actually suffer more intensely from cognitive dissonance. Why? Because it's not only the partner you have to reconcile. It's the version of yourself who chose him, trusted him, and defended him. And that inner fracture is what keeps so many of us stuck.

Who was I in that Airbnb? The accomplished professional who knew better? Or the woman laughing off being physically intimidated because we were all drunk? The therapist who could spot manipulation a mile away? Or the girlfriend making excuses for increasingly erratic behavior? This is why we stay longer than we should. It's not because of weakness. It's because our strength is working against us. Our natural optimism keeps us hoping things will improve. Our desire for harmony keeps us smoothing things over. Our conscientiousness keeps us committed even when everything inside us is screaming to run.

And here's the kicker: We often don't leave until our sense of self is so damaged that we can't maintain the illusion anymore. Until the cognitive dissonance becomes so painful that it finally breaks us.

But it doesn't have to be that way.

Understanding this pattern and recognizing how our Super Traits can become our super vulnerabilities is the first step to breaking this cycle. When you know that your natural inclination is to excuse bad behavior, you can catch yourself doing it. When you understand that your desire for harmony might be drowning out your instincts, you can choose to listen to the discord instead.

Because here's what I wish I'd known that New Year's morning: Sometimes cognitive dissonance tries to protect you. Other times, it's your deepest wisdom trying to break through.

Maybe if I'd understood that then, I would have recognized that queasy feeling in my gut for what it was: not weakness, not rigidity, but my Super Traits finally trying to save me instead of sabotaging me.

THE POWER IN TRUSTING WHAT YOU KNOW

My body remembers what my mind tried to forget.

Even now, years later, describing that mosh pit moment makes my stomach clench. That reaction is wisdom, not anxiety or trauma. My body knew the truth before my brain would let me see it.

So, these days, I listen.

When I meet someone new and that familiar unease creeps in, that subtle discord between their words and actions, the way their fun carries an edge of aggression, how their eyes go flat when they drink, I no longer write a dissertation in my head explaining it away. I don't wonder if I'm being too rigid or untrusting. I give weight to my perceptions. I let myself sit with the discomfort instead of rushing to smooth it over. These instincts kept trying to protect me with Tyler. Unfortunately, I just wasn't ready to hear them.

That's the real freedom that comes with understanding cognitive dissonance: You stop fighting yourself. When your Super Traits start sending up flares, when your natural conscientiousness recoils at someone's inconsistency, when your emotional intelligence picks up on subtle shifts in behavior, you don't have to override those signals. That's because they're not obstacles to connection. They make up your innate security system.

I used to think my sensitivity to others' emotions was a weakness. Now I understand it's a superpower. But it's only a superpower if I use it to protect myself instead of trying to heal everyone else. My ability to see the best in people is a gift. But it doesn't require me to stay when someone shows me who they really are.

The women who come to me for therapy often say the same thing: "I should have known better." But that's not true. We did know better. We just didn't trust what we knew. That's what changes when you understand how these relationships work. You stop seeing red flags as challenges to overcome. You stop trying to find the real version of someone beneath their chaos. That's because you now accept that if someone can switch from warm to cold that easily, the switch itself is who they are.

My Super Traits haven't changed. I'm still optimistic about

human nature. I still value harmony in relationships. I still want to see the best in people. But now I understand that those qualities are gifts to be given selectively, not vulnerabilities to be exploited.

Now, when I think back to that New Year's in New York, I don't blame myself for not leaving immediately. Understanding the pattern doesn't mean beating yourself up for not seeing it sooner. But I do smile at how differently I'd handle it now. The first signs of instability is the first hint that someone could flip from jovial to threatening or from attentive to aloof. I now honor that flutter of uncertainty in my gut. Instead of pushing for more closeness to prove my doubts wrong, I step back and give myself space to listen to what my body is trying to tell me.

The darkness that descended when everything fell apart with Tyler is slowly lifting and I'm learning to cherish my light in ways I couldn't before. When you've watched someone try to dim your shine, you develop a fierce protectiveness of it. I'm not fully healed, but I don't know if any of us ever are. Nonetheless, I'm reclaiming the strength that was always there, the wisdom that tried to warn me. This time, I'm listening.

That's the real gift of understanding these patterns. Yes, you learn to avoid toxic relationships, but in the process, you reclaim your strength. The traits that made you vulnerable transform into your greatest protection once you learn to honor them instead of override them.

You don't have to dull your shine. You just have to stop giving it away to people who don't deserve it.

REAL TALK: STOP JUSTIFYING. START SEEING.

You'd think that after going through this before, I would have seen it coming.

But these relationships are deceptive. They don't all look the same at first. Some start with red flags waving in your face. Others start with a Christmas morning in matching pajamas, a perfectly calibrated love story designed to make you feel safe.

And that's what makes them so dangerous.

This is why women like me and like you are particularly vulnerable. *Because of* our Super Traits. We're not blind. We're not weak. We're wired to see the best in people.

For a long time, I didn't see the full pattern either. I knew I kept landing in relationships that left me exhausted, confused, and carrying the weight alone. But I didn't have the words for it: Dark Tetrad, disordered character, pathology. Those labels came much later, after I started doing the work.

Back then, I only knew that something always felt off. And once I started to connect the dots to past boyfriends, to Tyler, it was like the curtain finally got pulled back. These weren't random bad picks. They were variations of the same blueprint I'd been unconsciously familiar with my whole life. It's why we don't run at the first sign of trouble. It's why we justify, minimize, and work harder to fix things. We're wired to create order from disorder, to tackle challenges head-on, and to take on difficult projects and see them through. It's why we succeed in our careers, why we're the ones people rely on, and why we're so good at fixing things.

But a man isn't supposed to be a project. A relationship isn't something you build alone, bending and reshaping yourself to make it work. With the right person, a relationship is a kind of project, but one you build together. One where both people are equally invested, where the work strengthens you instead of breaking you down. Where the whole is greater than the sum of its parts.

But this wasn't that.

When all the effort, adjusting, and responsibility falls entirely on you, that's not a partnership. That's a slow erosion of your values, your peace, and yourself.

That's why cognitive dissonance is so powerful. When someone contradicts the story you've already written about them, your brain doesn't sound an alarm. It starts doing damage control. And that's where selective exposure comes in:

It's just the alcohol talking.

It was just one bad night.

Maybe I'm being too rigid.

When reality starts contradicting what we want to believe, we do what human brains are wired to do: we filter. We seek out the evidence that reinforces our preferred truth (he's loving, he's good to me, this will pass) and unconsciously downplay the rest (the way he grabbed me wasn't that bad, everyone gets drunk sometimes, at least he apologized). We justify their behavior. We justify staying.

It's not stupidity. It's survival.

But how do you break free?

Stop chasing closure. We think that if we just gather enough information, we'll be able to make a clean, logical decision. But your brain isn't struggling because it lacks information. It's struggling because it doesn't want to integrate the information it already has. Stop waiting for some final piece of proof that makes it impossible to stay. If you're looking for a reason to go, you already have it.

Resist the urge to cherry-pick the good. When you feel stuck in a cycle of doubt, write down both the best and worst moments of your relationship. Patterns will emerge, and you'll see that the real him isn't just the guy who made you feel safe on Christmas. He's also the guy who knocked you down in an Airbnb and laughed about it. They are both him.

Flip the script. If a friend told you the same story about her partner, would you tell her to stay? Would you say, "Well, he was great two weeks ago, so maybe this isn't so bad?" Probably not. So, what story are you telling yourself?

Here's what I wish I had known back then: The moment you start explaining away someone's behavior instead of simply experiencing it for what it is, you've already begun the process of betraying yourself.

That's the real red flag. And that's the one you can't afford to ignore.

Let's Reflect

That Christmas morning felt like safety, a warm, familiar place I thought I could trust. But beneath the surface, there were cracks I chose not to see. Betraying yourself starts small but compounds over time. The courage to face reality honestly is the first step toward reclaiming your power and peace.

Super Traits He Targeted:

- Desire for harmony

- Dependability

- Desire to be truly understood

- Tendency to question self before suspecting others

Red Flags That Felt Like Safety:

- Introducing me to his family & friends very early on

- Love bombing and constant praise

 ## Journal Coaching Moment

Find a quiet space, take a deep breath, and let yourself reflect honestly, without judgment or pressure. This is your space to explore, not to be perfect.

Can you remember a time you felt swept up in someone's charm, only to later see cracks in their story?

Did their words match their actions? If not, what tipped the scales first—the shift in their behavior or your changing feelings?

What felt genuine, and what started to raise doubts?

How did your instincts respond—did you listen or push them aside?

6

The Mental Mess of Mixed Signals

JOURNAL ENTRY

It's easy to look at the signs now and say, "Well, duh-there were red flags everywhere." But when you're in it, it unfolds so differently. The red flags turn into pink flags. There's so much I should have questioned. But I didn't.

The plane landed and I exhaled, as if I could let New York go with it. Tyler scrolled casually through his phone beside me, seemingly unbothered by the chaos he'd starred in throughout the trip. I stole a sideways glance at him, searching for any lingering sign of the man who had pinned me down in our Airbnb, whose eyes had gone vacant in that terrifying moment, but there was nothing.

He caught me looking, flashed that magnetic smile, and just like that, the knot in my stomach loosened. Maybe I was overreacting. After all, doesn't everyone have a night they'd rather forget after too many drinks? I know I have! And this was New York, that chaotic, intoxicating city that has a way of bringing out people's wild side.

"Hey," he said, as we waited for the seatbelt sign to turn off. "Let's grab Chinese on the way home, have some wine, and binge-watch a show. Just relax, yeah?"

And just like that, we were back to normal. The perfect boyfriend had returned, as if the moody, aggressive version of him had been left behind in Manhattan. Tyler was Tyler again; all easy charm and playful texts that made it seem like we were still wrapped up in something rare and electric.

We made it home. The Kung Pao chicken was open on the kitchen counter, and Duke, his Doberman, circled our legs excitedly; the discomfort of the trip had already begun to fade. This was the real Tyler. Attentive, thoughtful, present. The other version was just an anomaly. A blip. It was easier to see New York as nothing more than a wild, booze-fueled wrong turn off an otherwise steady path. We were fine. And yet, something in me was already side-eyeing the whole situation, waiting for the other shoe to drop.

Weeks passed, and life settled back into a comfortable rhythm. Tyler had made himself at home. His dog roamed my yard, his projects cluttered my garage, and his clothes remained neatly folded in my dresser. Tyler still had his apartment in Atlanta, but for all practical purposes, he lived with me. It felt natural, like we were building something real.

Then came that night at our local Mexican restaurant. We were having margaritas, looking through old photos of his motocross racing days on his phone, when I noticed the red and white icon of Tinder on his home screen.

"Why do you still have that?" I asked, my throat suddenly tight.

Tyler blinked, baffled, as if seeing something he was certain didn't exist. "Oh, my bad! I thought I'd deleted that."

"We agreed to be exclusive months ago," I said, working to keep my voice steady. "Why would you still have that on your phone?"

"Honestly? I just forgot," he said, his tone light, unbothered. "I haven't used it since we met. You know that!"

I watched his face closely, searching for a flicker of guilt, a tell, anything that might betray him. But there was nothing. No anxiety, no defensiveness, just a calm certainty that made me question my reaction.

"I'll delete it now," he said, already doing so with a few taps. "See? Gone." Then he smirked. "Don't be that girl. You know better than that."

But something about the exchange stuck with me.

"You keep your eye where you want to go, not where you are," he'd once told me about motocross racing. So, I threw it back at him. "If you're really moving forward with me, why keep something that points in the opposite direction?"

He tilted his head, considering. "Huh. I never really thought about it like that. But you're right. That makes sense."

He made it seem like I'd just given him some deep insight. Like he was grateful. Like this was progress.

But later that night, as he slept beside me, I realized he hadn't actually answered the question. If Tyler truly intended to be exclusive, why keep the app at all?

That Friday, Tyler went on a trip with his father, leaving his new smartwatch charging on my nightstand. Late Saturday, the screen flashed to life, and my eyes snapped toward it.

"Can't wait to see those big titties in that extra-small shirt," the text read.

My blood ran cold, my heart raced, my stomach tightened. This wasn't an old message. The time stamp was from yesterday. *Are you kidding me?* I then grabbed the watch and scrolled through more messages. There were others, to women I'd never heard of. Reminiscing about hookups. Commenting on bodies. All while he was supposedly committed to me.

Nope. Absolutely Not.

I didn't say anything to him then as he wasn't there to hear it. I called my best friend instead and let the tears and fury rip. But my mind was already made up.

By the time Tyler walked through my door Sunday, I didn't need any more proof. No arguments, no explanations, no pleading would change what I'd seen with my own eyes. The switch had flipped. I was angry.

"Get out of my house," I yelled.

THE WAR BETWEEN LOGIC AND INSTINCT

I thought the decision was final, but the battle was just beginning between my head and my heart—I wanted to believe him.

I'd always prided myself on my intuition. I told my clients the same thing I told my friends: When something feels off, it probably is. Your brain just hasn't caught up to what your gut already knows. Yet here I was, ignoring the alarms blaring in my own head.

This is what people misunderstand about women who get trapped in these dynamics. It's not blindness, and it's certainly not stupidity. It's a battle between logic and instinct, hope and unease. And when you have the Super Traits, you've built a life on being competent, loyal, and understanding, and you don't just assume the worst. You ask questions. You seek clarity.

But Dark Tetrad individuals, those who lack conscience, who move through life without the burden of guilt or genuine remorse, exploit that tendency. If you need a modern reference point, watch the Diddy documentary. These aren't rare cases. As Dr. Robert D. Hare, creator of the Psychopathy Checklist, explains: "There's a class of individuals who have been around forever, found in every culture and walk of life. Everybody has met these people, been deceived and manipulated by them. These charming yet deadly individuals have a clinical name: psychopaths. Their hallmark is a stunning lack of conscience; their game is self-gratification at the other person's expense."

Psychopaths may be the most extreme example, but they aren't the only ones who fit the bill. Many low-conscience individuals, whether they fall on the spectrum of psychopathy, narcissism, or just plain selfishness, are skilled at manipulation. They don't second-guess themselves. They don't experience the same inner conflict. And that's precisely why they're so convincing. While you're busy weighing the evidence, they're already onto their next move.

That's what makes Dark Tetrad personalities so dangerous. Charm is their vehicle. Control is the destination. They shift seamlessly between personas without hesitation, maintaining perfect composure because, for them, deception requires no effort. There's no contradiction, no cognitive dissonance, no emotional weight behind the mask they put on. As a result, only the target feels the whiplash.

When I saw Tinder still on his phone, my stomach tightened. There it was, proof of something, or maybe nothing. My mind scrambled to fill in the blanks before he even had a chance to answer. Maybe it was a remnant from before we met? A meaningless oversight? Or an actual betrayal?

The human brain craves cognitive equilibrium. That's because we resolve contradictions in whatever way feels the most stable and the least threatening. And Tyler made it easy. No hesitation, no defensiveness. Just an easy smile, a light chuckle, an "Oh, dang, I thought I deleted that months ago." His calm felt like confirmation, not of his guilt, but of my overreaction.

Most people show signs when they lie. They exhibit nervous gestures, give inconsistent details, and show cracks in their composure. Not men like Tyler. With low cognitive load, his deception was effortless. Tyler wasn't scrambling for an explanation. He already had one. Tyler deleted the app right in front of me, like a magician making the evidence disappear. He said, "See?" turning the phone to me. "Gone." And just like that, Tyler neutralized the issue. And as a result, his place in my home, his increasing presence in my life, were all left unthreatened.

This wasn't accidental. Sandra L. Brown notes that low-conscience individuals often accelerate domestic entanglements to make leaving more difficult. His constant presence and belongings gradually finding permanent spots in my space felt natural at the time. In reality, it was a carefully laid foundation. With each passing week, the cost of walking away for me became higher, not just emotionally, but practically.

And besides, it felt good to have him back, to slip into the familiar rhythm of warmth and affection, to convince myself that the worst was behind us. That's because the push and pull of intermittent reinforcement, where rewards come unpredictably rather than consistently, creates an addiction-like response in the brain. Like a gambler at a slot machine, I found myself constantly waiting for the next moment when Tyler would return to being the perfect boyfriend. When that moment came, the relief was so intense that it overrode all the red flags that had accumulated.

So, I stayed the course, told myself I needed more proof, some concrete reason to walk away. And that's the final trap of Super Traits: When trust is broken, we don't assume we've been deceived. We instead assume we're missing something.

BREAKING FREE FROM THE PSYCHOLOGICAL TRAP

When I tried to walk away from Tyler, it wasn't because I'd become someone else. It was because I was having flashbacks on who I was.

Breaking free starts with recognizing the traits they exploited and using them, on your terms, to rebuild. Here's how:

REFRAME YOUR INTUITION

Start treating your discomfort as data, rather than doubt. Those moments when something feels off, but you can't articulate why? That's your subconscious processing information your conscious mind hasn't caught up to yet.

When I saw those messages on Tyler's watch, I had a moment of perfect clarity. But I knew from experience that doubt would return.

Your Super Traits are misapplied strengths, not weaknesses. The goal isn't to become harder or colder, but to become more discerning about who deserves access to your gifts.

· ·

Breaking free doesn't always look like a Beyoncé-level power move. Sometimes it's unfollowing him at 2 a.m., knowing this time, you won't go back. It's canceling the dinner plans you know will wreck your peace and choosing to stay home by yourself. It's the steady work of learning to trust yourself again and of recognizing that the same traits that made you vulnerable are also your greatest strengths when properly directed.

Your capacity for empathy, your integrity, your ability to see the best in others aren't flaws. They're superpowers to be protected.

THE ROAD NOT YET TAKEN

Sometimes I wonder how different my path might have been if I'd walked away that night and never looked back. If I'd packed his things, changed the locks, and protected my heart before it suffered deeper wounds.

But that wasn't my journey.

I surrendered several more years of my life and drained my savings to fully comprehend that with people like Tyler, there is no redemption story. No amount of understanding, patience, or love will make the mask of decency become their true face. Their patterns aren't slip-ups or bad habits. They're the core of who they are, buried under a well-practiced act.

What I didn't know then, and what took me far too long to accept, is that breaking free is rarely as clean as a single moment of clarity. That's because the promises would come. The tearful confessions. The sudden interest in therapy. The completely reformed man. The supposed breakthroughs that seemed too "insightful" to be a manipulation. Each time, hope would flicker back to life, and each time, it would be extinguished more painfully than before. Can you recall a time when someone's "breakthrough" or sudden self-awareness felt real only to be followed by the same toxic behavior?

I was going to therapy before Tyler arrived, working toward sobriety, toward healing from my mother's death, toward reclaiming myself after years of shouldering everyone else's burdens. My DUI should have been my wake-up call. Instead, Tyler's chaos provided the perfect excuse to delay my own healing.

Had I left earlier, maybe I would have found my way to sobriety with less damage done. Perhaps, I would have grieved my mother and my divorce without the constant static of relationship chaos. I possibly would have rebuilt my life with fewer scars.

But I might also have missed the insight that finally allowed me to break the cycle completely. It took this particular devastation, this complete unraveling, for me to finally see the truth: Men like Tyler aren't drawn to weakness. They're drawn to strength. To women who are capable, accomplished, and deeply loyal. The kind of women who don't walk away easily.

And yet, when we talk about victims of these relationships, we don't talk about women like me. Women like you. We hear about the traumatized, the insecure, the codependent, the ones with "daddy issues" or low self-esteem. But what about the confident, smart, educated, successful women who had their lives together in every other way?

That's the part no one warns us about. That's the betrayal that cuts even deeper than Tyler's manipulation. The fact that I had spent decades preparing myself for the wrong threats. I was never taught that my strength, my loyalty, my ability to see the best in people could be weaponized against me. That my greatest assets could make me a target.

I now move through the world with eyes that can spot manipulation before it has a chance to take root. My Super Traits remain intact, but they're now guarded by boundaries that took years to build. However, you can establish them much sooner.

The clarity I've gained didn't come cheap. But it did come.

You shouldn't have to learn this the hard way. You shouldn't have to be stripped down to nothing to understand the game you never agreed to play.

The difference between my story and yours is that you still have time to write a different ending.

REAL TALK: NO MORE MENTAL GYMNASTICS

You've already had the thought. That nagging whisper that something isn't right. That something doesn't add up. You tell yourself you need more proof. Something definitive. But that moment rarely comes.

That's the trick of intermittent reinforcement. It keeps you chasing the next good moment, the next version of him that reminds you why you fell for him in the first place. And that's why walking away feels impossible. Not because you don't know something is wrong, but because your brain has been conditioned to override your own doubt.

So, let's short-circuit that cycle right now.

Flip the script. If a friend told you the exact story you're living, what would you say to her? Would you tell her to stay? Would you encourage her to wait, and see? Or would you tell her that she deserves better, that she already knows what she needs to do? If you'd tell her to run, then what is holding you back from leaving?

Plan your exit before you need it. The best time to prepare for your escape isn't in the middle of a crisis, it's before the storm hits. Even if you're not ready to leave, even if part of you still hopes things will change, start putting things in place now:

- *Secure independent financial access.* Open a separate bank account if you don't already have one. Start setting aside small amounts of money that you can easily access.

- *Gather important documents.* Your passport, your ID, anything tied to shared assets, and have copies stored somewhere safe.

- *Assemble a "go-bag" for your car.* Pack a change of clothes, extra medication, spare toiletries, and cash. Planning ahead ensures if things escalate, you will be prepared to leave quickly.

- *Identify your support system.* Who are the people in your life who see the truth? Who won't minimize your experience or talk you into staying? Keep them close.

If you don't need the plan, great. But if you do? You'll be glad you didn't wait.

Stop playing the game. Intermittent reinforcement is a psychological trap; one designed to keep you stuck in a pattern of chasing a dream that was never real to begin with. Yes, the cycle is intoxicating, but there's only one way to win:

You stop playing.

No more justifications. No more bending reality to fit the person you wish he was. No more explaining away the things that would make you run if you saw them happening to someone else.

Honestly, if you're waiting for enough pain to push you out, it *will* come. The only question is, how much are you willing to endure before you listen to what you already know?

Remember this: your empathy, loyalty, and willingness to believe in the best version of someone aren't flaws. These Super Traits define your strength. They don't need to be changed; they need to be safeguarded.

LET'S REFLECT

That moment on the plane, I thought, *"See? He's sweet. He's trying."*

He wasn't trying. He was manufacturing emotional intimacy to use as currency. The warmth, the affection, the cozy plans? That wasn't comfort for my sake. It was control, disguised as connection, for his sake. That's how smart women stay longer than they should.

Super Traits He Targeted:

- Altruism

- Loyalty

- Ability to forgive

Red Flags That Looked Like Normalcy:

- Dismissing concerns with calm logic

- Minimizing and justifying

- Offering breadcrumbs of affection while calling it connection

JOURNAL COACHING MOMENT

Find a quiet space, take a deep breath, and let yourself

reflect honestly, without judgment or pressure. This is your space to explore, not to be perfect.

Have you ever felt relief after a tense moment, only to realize later that relief was manipulation in disguise?

Did someone ever say something that made you question your instincts, even though your body was screaming something else?

What was the cost of believing the version of them they offered, instead of trusting what you saw with your own eyes?

7

Funding the Facade

LETTER FROM TYLER
We can have an even more incredible relationship than the one we have had. I will confide in you. I will finish this house and all projects I've neglected.

We were a freaking rom-com movie.

By late 2019, Tyler had officially moved into my home. The house felt full with his dog by the fireplace, his books on my shelves, his energy in every room. My place had always been peaceful, but now it pulsed with a new kind of hope.

Three months earlier, I'd caught him texting other women. Two months before that, he'd vanished during our New York trip and returned belligerent and wasted. But on that November evening, Tyler sat by the firepit scrolling through his laptop like a man on a mission.

"I found it!" he called from the porch.

"Found what?" I asked, hands slick from chopping vegetables.

"Your engagement ring."

He then turned his screen toward me and revealed a black diamond kite-shaped solitaire platinum band. Unique, bold. Just like me.

"Twelve thousand," he said, proud of himself. "That's what you deserve."

Twelve. Thousand. Dollars. Far more expensive than what I was expecting.

"That's...a lot," I said, trying to sound touched, not alarmed. All the while thinking, *"You're saving for this while I'm bankrolling everything else?"*

"I'm working for it," he said. "Every extra project. Every side freelance gig, it's all going toward our future."

He looked so earnest, so sincere. And maybe he believed himself. I watched him, so sure, so full of love, and I wanted to match that energy. But some part of me stayed slightly offstage, waiting to see if the scene would hold.

At this point, we'd been together for a year, and Tyler had officially moved in the week before Thanksgiving. We were playing house, splitting the bills, cooking together, and settling into our routines. I wanted so badly to believe it was real. The truth was, I wanted to be married again. I loved the feeling of having a teammate, that us-against-the-world thing.

Then COVID hit, and the whole world shut down. What should've felt claustrophobic turned cozy. Our forced togetherness became a kind of fever dream. I'd built a career; now I was building a life. We converted my porch into a sunroom so we could both work from home. We snuggled under blankets, watching movies projected onto the side of the house while the firepit crackled between us. Then, after months of late-night snacks and lazy evenings on the couch, we decided to clean things up. I bought us matching Cannondale Mountain bikes. We vowed to eat better, move more, and spend more time outdoors.

It felt good to feel stable. This wasn't the early love bombing. This felt earned. Real. *He'd changed*; I told myself. *We'd grown together.* My vigilance dulled. Hyperawareness faded. I could finally exhale.

"I never thought I'd want marriage again," he said quietly, his hand resting warm and heavy across my stomach. "But with you, I want it all."

And I believed him. So, I leaned in, deeper, harder. All in. I wasn't just investing emotionally anymore. I was putting my name on the line. We had the same vision: camping with friends, bonfires, a mountain forever home. So, by that summer, we found a piece of land in Tennessee, our supposed "forever spot." I bought it without hesitation and put him on the deed.

That was the next logical step in our blueprint. And he took to it immediately, clearing trees, dragging lumber, sketching tiny home blueprints. I'd watch him work in the heat, shirtless and full of purpose, thinking, *this is What I Think It Means to have a man.*

I was making six figures and had worked hard to get there. He was contributing through sweat equity. I covered the bikes, the land, the trips, and the sunroom conversion. But men like Tyler will do just enough. And if your love language is acts of service, like mine, it's intoxicating. However, Tyler was getting comfortable. Too comfortable. The man who once made grand declarations and performed devotion like it was theater had started to relax into the role of expecting the perks of partnership without contributing to the weight of it. I had created stability, and he moved through it like it was owed to him. And that's when the shift began.

A knot was forming.

The first digs were subtle. "You know you feel better when you're skinnier," he'd say. "I just want you to be healthy." Meanwhile, he could no longer fit into his pants.

"You're a corporate badass, but you can't nail two boards together?" Right, because I didn't spend my childhood shadowing his dad on job sites.

These hurtful pokes were always followed by a grin. And if he sensed the sting, a quick, "Chill out, it's a joke." Followed by another blow: "You're too sensitive," he'd say as he tilted his head like I was a cute little idiot.

When I asked him to pitch in financially on big items, he'd remind me again that he was "saving for the ring." Like I should be grateful for his non-financial contributions. Meanwhile, I was funding this whole enterprise.

Our sex life was healthy, but it started to feel transactional. Unless we fought, then he'd flip the switch, go tender and passionate. He'd look deep into my eyes and whisper, "I cherish you. I love you." But his tenderness was never consistent. Just another strategy he'd deploy just long enough to keep me. A dopamine hit. A reset button to draw me in.

It's easy to see the pattern now. At the time, I shrugged it off. Told myself, *everyone slips sometimes. Nobody's perfect. We all have bad days.* Yet every time I made excuses, I gave him more runway. But the late summer trip to Florida was where that runway ran out.

We were camping while working remotely. Beach by day, laptops by night. On our last night, we stopped at the bar across from our rental. He was buzzed and I felt he was flirting with the bartender. I wasn't worried. He was always like that. After we had a couple of bourbons, I decided to head back.

"Just one more drink," Tyler said. "I'll be back within the hour."

I kissed him and said, "Be good." Then headed to bed so I'd be rested for an early work meeting.

I woke up at 6 a.m. Alone. No Tyler. No texts. No missed calls. His phone went straight to voicemail. I tried the police. The hospitals. Every dark place your mind goes when you think something awful has happened, my mind went there too.

By 9:30 a.m., I'd canceled my work meetings and extended our stay. I was sick with panic. Until he strolled in barefoot. Hair matted with sand and sweat. And smelling like a brewery.

"I grabbed a bottle after you left," he said. "Went down to the beach. Drank. Phone died. I must've passed out."

That was it. No apology. No concern for my fear or my job. No awareness that disappearing all night might actually affect someone else. No conscience.

At first, I felt numb and hollow. Then came the rage. I was furious that I'd canceled meetings, lied to my work about why I canceled, extended our stay, and called hospitals searching for him. I was furious that this entitled jerk came strolling in barefoot, carefree, like my panic meant nothing. Like I meant nothing. For months, he's been screwing with my head. Now he was screwing with my career, my ability to focus, and my livelihood. But I kept covering for him. For him and for myself.

A BLUEPRINT FOR NOWHERE

I think by then, Tyler knew I needed more from him. More steadiness, more certainty. So, he sold me his dream of a shared home . Said we'd renovate it together and do something cool with the land. Said it would be our project, our beginning. Green pastures for days. The old horse farm stretched out around us, soft and open, the kind of land that makes you breathe deeper without realizing it. Our long gravel driveway was flanked by trees, their limbs arching overhead like they were blessing the place. It was a few minutes from his parents' house, thirty miles from Atlanta, but it felt like a different world.

There's a specific kind of heartbreak that doesn't look like heartbreak at all. It looks like loyalty. Investment. A future built from shared blueprints and borrowed promises.

The romantic gestures, the future talk, and the ring shopping were all part of the same cycle: love bomb, devalue, disappear. Over and over.

I looked around at the life we were supposedly building and finally asked the question I should've asked from the start: *Whose blueprint are we following?*

Somewhere along the way, I'd drifted from my values. Even my work, something I never took lightly, had started to slip. And the truth was, I'd let it happen for him.

Tyler said the right things. Promised the right things. Played the part so well that I started playing it too. I ignored what I knew because I wanted to believe him, because sadly, belief feels better than betrayal. Especially when you've already poured so much of yourself into the fantasy.

But belief without evidence is a dangerous currency. And when someone keeps cashing in on your hope without delivering a return, that's not a relationship. That's a con job.

I didn't stay with Tyler because I was weak. I stayed because I was convinced I could make our relationship work. That's the difference people don't talk about: the difference between delusion and determination.

But the pattern was already there. The cycle was already running. I just hadn't admitted to myself that I was the only one doing the building. And if I'm being honest, I was lying to myself. How the lies you tell yourself slowly erode your soul.

Women like me don't leave at the first sign of trouble. We adapt. We problem-solve. We wait for potential to catch up with reality. And that's exactly what men like Tyler count on.

You're familiar with Brown's research on Super Traits by now, how those elevated levels of empathy, loyalty, and conscientiousness make certain women particularly vulnerable to manipulation. My clinical training should have been an advantage, but when my Super Traits collided with Tyler's Dark Tetrad characteristics, textbook knowledge couldn't compete with emotional investment. Especially when the manipulator wears a flannel shirt and builds you an epic sunroom.

Tyler knew how to keep me hooked. When I started to pull away, he upped the charm: "I'm saving for your ring." "We're building a life." "I've never felt this way about anyone." Psychologists call this Future Faking, dangling elaborate promises of commitment to distract from what's not working now. It creates the illusion of progress while nothing actually changes. It buys time. It resets the hope cycle. And when your strengths include loyalty and emotional endurance, it's the perfect trap.

Part of me knew something was off. But I'm human, like you, and wanted to believe that love would prevail. And that's the emotional trick. You start adjusting yourself to accommodate the illusion. You double down when you should walk away. You rationalize the red flags because the dream is so beautiful, so close, so workable, and because the manipulator is so skilled at playing the part. But there's a fine line between hope and denial, especially when your strength lies in seeing the best in people and believing you can weather the hard parts. Have you ever felt that blur yourself?

The longer I stayed in that space, the more my tolerance turned into permission. What started as grace slowly became an open door for disrespect. And once that door cracked open, the digs slipped in. He made jabs about my weight and slights about not knowing how to use power tools. They were slipped in, wrapped in jokes or "helpful" concerns. A coward's ways of airing grievances. And the jabs landed. Every time.

When Tyler smirked at me like I was cute for being so dumb, I didn't think, *this is a pattern of erosion designed to make me feel incompetent.* I instead thought, *maybe I am bad at this. Maybe I should try harder.*

In reality, those remarks I became increasingly accustomed to were Covert Abuse, indirect and dismissive behavior that coerces you into participating in your own diminishment. The alternative would mean acknowledging that someone you love is deliberately chipping away at your self-worth. And when your Super Traits include empathy and optimism, you'll bend over backward to give them the benefit of the doubt:

Tyler wasn't criticizing me. No, he was "helping."

He wasn't dismissive. No, he was "direct."

He wasn't eroding my confidence. No, he was "keeping it real."

That's how women like us get stuck. We feel the harm, but it doesn't fit our view of human nature. We give more, love harder, and assume the manipulator is doing their best to reciprocate. So, to leave would feel like failure, not escape. Especially when you've built a career on solving complex problems. Especially when your identity is tied to being someone who finishes what she starts. When effort is your love language, quitting feels like giving up.

But effort is not the same as intimacy. And commitment doesn't mean staying somewhere that's killing you. The real issue isn't our longevity in these relationships. The problem is that we've been taught to see our endurance as a virtue in all contexts, and men with Dark Tetrad traits know exactly how to capitalize on that.

They don't always need to isolate you. Or yell. Or hit. Although many do.

All they need to do is sell you a future, keep you working for it, and make you question your instincts until you're too invested to leave.

That's the blueprint.

And until you recognize it as a pattern, you'll keep trying to build something that was never meant to stand.

RECLAIMING YOUR VISION

So, what do you do when you realize you're living inside someone else's blueprint?

You take a step back.

You study it.

And then you start drawing your own.

Here's what I had to learn the hard way, so maybe you don't have to spend years of your life trying to make a broken foundation hold:

NAME THE PATTERN

When I finally saw Tyler clearly, it wasn't a single moment. It was the moment I realized I was stuck in a rerun. Same script, same ending, new excuses.

Future promises → early effort → fizzle → manipulation → reset.

Ring shopping. Tiny home plans. Grand declarations. Every one of them bought him more time, more forgiveness, more access to my energy, my body, and my wallet.

This went beyond turbulence. It was choreography and a pattern, one that began long before I showed up in Tyler's story. It showed up in his earlier relationships. And if I am being honest, it showed up in my earlier relationships, too. Researchers at Bowling Green University call this Relationship Churning, breaking up and getting back together again and again. Their study found that people in these cycles are twice as likely to experience verbal and physical abuse. And when your partner has Dark Tetrad traits, that risk gets even higher.

This is the kind of harm that builds quietly, until you can't unsee it.

And power comes the moment you stop asking, *"Why did he do that today?"* and start saying, *"This is what he does."*

STICK TO THE FACTS

Start tracking behaviors, inconsistencies, and financial expenditures whether in a notebook or in the notes app on your phone. Over time, you'll start recognizing the patterns that reveal someone's true nature and intentions. The more you document it, the harder it becomes for anyone, including yourself, to rewrite the story. I call it sticking to the facts: What's true? What do I know?

TRUST THE WAY IT FEELS

You don't need hard proof to walk away. You just need to start listening to the alarm that's been sounding inside you all along.

When Tyler disappeared overnight, it was a slap in my face. Like my time, my work, and my fear didn't matter.

When he made digs about my weight, my stomach clenched.

When he tilted his head like I was cute for being so dumb, my whole body shrank. Those were signals.

And that's one of the hardest parts of these relationships, recognizing that it's a pattern, not a string of isolated moments. Believing that takes a kind of self-trust that's easy to lose when you're being manipulated. Unfortunately, you lost that trust at the cost of your mental health. Research on covert abuse shows that sarcasm, dismissiveness, and disguised criticism can do real harm, sometimes more than overt aggression. But they're harder to call out, and easier to excuse. Especially when you've been trained to work through discomfort.

In the corporate world, you hear it all the time: "What you put in is what you get out." "There's no substitute for hustle." "Work hard and you'll rise." So, you keep pushing. You override the knot in your stomach with the same determination you've used for tough meetings and impossible deadlines, treating the discomfort as just another challenge to push through.

So, every time Tyler said, "You know you feel better when you're skinnier," I didn't hear cruelty. I heard a challenge. I told myself he meant well. I pushed the feeling down.

But he wasn't helping me. He was managing me. And every time I ignored that knot in my gut, I betrayed myself and handed him more control.

That discomfort matters. Those physical responses matter. They're part of the data. And they're worth trusting.

REFRAME THE LOYALTY TRAP

Loyalty kept me standing on that land long after the future we imagined had fallen apart.

I kept making excuses for his inconsistent behaviors. I kept hoping the steady, attentive man I initially fell in love with would become the norm rather than the exception.

That kind of loyalty can feel noble. It can also become a leash. I was raised to show up, to work hard, and to stick things out. And those traits serve you well when you're with someone healthy. But when you're with someone disordered, they become the exact traits that keep you stuck.

Dark Tetrad personalities feed off external validation. Studies show they'll keep performing as long as they're being seen, praised, and rewarded. But when attention fades, or they decide they're owed more, they drop the act. And this discarding comes in many forms: cheating, minimizing, pulling away, going silent, and making you feel like you're the problem. Each one is designed to destabilize you while they secure their next supply.

So, ask yourself: Am I staying because I feel secure here? Or because I've already given so much that leaving feels like losing? Your empathy and endurance are real strengths. But when you hand them to someone who exploits them, they become the reason you stay stuck.

REBUILD WITH SELF-COMPASSION—REDIRECT YOUR LOYALTY

If conscientiousness can become your investigative superpower, then loyalty, rightly directed, can become your greatest strength in healing.

Women with Super Traits excel at being devoted to others. We show up. We stay. We fight. We honor our commitments. But what would happen if you channeled even a fraction of that fierce loyalty toward yourself? That's what self-compassion truly is. It's not self-indulgence. It's not weakness. It's the disciplined practice of turning your loyalty inward and being as devoted to your well-being as you've been to everyone else's. It's treating yourself with the same dignity, respect, and care you so readily give to others.

Dr. Kristin Neff's research on self-compassion shows it serves as a powerful protective factor for women trapped in toxic cycles. It interrupts the shame spiral of *"I should have known better"* and replaces it with *"I did what I could with what I knew. And now I know better."*

Start here:

- What would loyalty to myself look like today?

- What boundary would I encourage my best friend to set in this situation?

- What acts of care would I insist upon for someone I love who's been through what I have?

Your staying was loyalty in action, not weakness. Self-compassion helps you see this truth. And leaving isn't failure. It's loyalty re-routed.

BUILD YOUR OWN BLUEPRINT

Tyler sold me a future so I'd ignore the present. He let me build everything while he played the part.

But I'm done chasing blueprints I didn't design. Now, I'm building one where I get to feel safe, seen, and free. Where my Super Traits don't become liabilities. Where loyalty is earned, not extracted.

Start small:

- One decision that centers your peace.

- One act of care for the woman who's carried it all.

- One truth you stop editing to make someone else more comfortable.

You already have the blueprint inside you.

You always did.

It's time to build it now.

THE WIN-WIN BLUEPRINT

What would change if you started building a life that works with or without him?

You wake up and check your bank account, the one with your name on it. The one you've been depositing into little by little, week by week. It doesn't matter whether the balance is large or modest. What matters is that it exists because it's yours.

Your name appears on the deed to your home. On your car title. On every important asset. You keep hard copies of key documents in a drawer that only you can access. Digital backups are password-protected. You know what you own, what you share, and where to find the things that matter.

Then one afternoon, when he suggests combining accounts to simplify things, you pause. There's a flicker of old pressure in your chest, a familiar urge to smooth things over. But it fades. You smile, thank him for the idea, and say the current setup works well for you. He pushes a little, but you don't flinch. Then the conversation moves on.

Weekends come and go. Some are shared meals cooked together, errands run in tandem, and an evening walk after dinner. Other days, you peel away. You sit alone at a coffee shop with a book and a playlist. You spend time with people who love you for reasons that have nothing to do with your romantic status. You take a breath that doesn't feel borrowed.

There was a time when none of this felt possible. When carving out space for yourself created conflict. When building a life outside of the relationship, triggered guilt, fear, or accusations of selfishness.

You save for things that matter to you now: a professional certification, a trip to Portugal, or a creative pursuit. Maybe he joins. Maybe he doesn't. But the plan still happens.

From the outside, your relationship might not look different. But inside, everything has changed. That's because you don't orbit around his moods. You don't build your calendar around his availability. You never apologize for your independence, your ambition, or the fact that your life feels full told with or without him in it.

When conflict shows up, it no longer knocks you flat. Your voice doesn't shake anymore when you speak up. If you cry, it's because something matters, not because something hurts. Now, when you rest, you actually rest, because there's no bracing for backlash.

You grow, and he grows with you. Or he doesn't. Either way, you're still building something solid.

Your career continues to progress.

Your savings account grows.

Your friendships deepen.

Your name stays on the documents.

Your energy goes where it's valued.

Your peace is no longer up for negotiation.

Your nervous system stops sounding the alarm every time you advocate for yourself. The panic that once rose with the thought of starting over starts to feel like clarity instead. You're no longer stuck in a blueprint that wasn't yours. You move through your days with your eyes open instead. You recognize red flags when they appear. You address issues directly. You set boundaries that protect your peace. You make decisions that serve your well-being while remaining open to compromise that doesn't diminish you.

If the relationship lasts, it lasts on new terms. If it ends, it ends without destroying you. And if the relationship holds, it holds because there's room for both of you to rise.

That's what healthy love does.

It invites growth.

It mirrors effort.

It doesn't shrink in the face of your strength.

This time, you're building something that doesn't require you to lose yourself to keep it standing. Because your future no longer depends on anyone else's blueprint. You're drafting your own now, and you trust the ground beneath your feet.

REAL TALK: AUDIT THE BLUEPRINT

This week, I want you to do one simple thing: Follow the money.

Grab a piece of paper and draw a line down the middle. On the left side, write "Mine." On the right side, write "Shared/His."

Under "Mine," list everything that's solely in your name:

- Bank accounts

- Property

- Investments

- Retirement funds

- Car titles

- Credit cards

Under "Shared/His," list everything that's in both names or just his:

- Joint accounts

- Shared property

- Merged investments

- Cosigned loans

Once you've made your lists, circle the items under "Mine" that you could access immediately in an emergency without anyone else's permission.

That's it. That's your task.

This exercise uses both Super Traits we talked about earlier. Your conscientiousness helps you collect the data objectively. Your redirected loyalty, toward yourself, helps you practice the self-compassion of acknowledging what's really yours.

Now, look at what you've circled. If the list feels solid, great. If it feels too thin, you now have clarity on exactly where to start building. Maybe that means opening a separate savings account. Maybe it means getting your name on a lease. Maybe it means taking photos of important documents.

Whether you're in a healthy relationship or a toxic one, loving and advocating for yourself will always serve you well. In a healthy partnership, this kind of awareness and independence actually strengthens the bond because you're choosing to be there, and not just because you're trapped by financial entanglement.

In an unhealthy situation, this simple audit might be the first step toward reclaiming your power. That's because even if your relationship status may change, your foundation should still be solid either way.

And now you get to build again. This time from truth, not illusion.

This time, using your own plans.

LET'S REFLECT

That morning, I thought, *He's a direct, blunt person. He didn't mean it in a mean way.* But I felt what he was doing was covert abuse, what seemed to me manipulation disguised as honesty and cruelty packaged as concern. That hollow feeling in my chest? That wasn't anxiety. That was my body telling the truth that my mind was too scared to face.

Pro tip: Your nervous system always knows. Listen sooner next time. That's how strong women get worn down.

Super Traits He Exploited:

- Loyalty

- High emotional endurance

- Conscientiousness

- Optimism

- Investment in growth

Red Flags That Looked Like a Future:

- Words with no real action at all, only the promise: "We're building a life."

- Ring shopping and future talk are classic future faking.

- Jokes that weren't really jokes.

- Disappearances followed by grand gestures.

📖 Journal Coaching Moment

Find a quiet space, take a deep breath, and let yourself reflect honestly, without judgment or pressure. This is your space to explore, not to be perfect.

Have you ever noticed yourself rationalizing someone else's bad behavior because you wanted the relationship to work?

What was the emotional, financial, and energetic cost of that rationalization?

Think back. Were there little comments or actions that didn't sit right, but you explained them away as stress, mis-communication, or "just how he is"?

And most importantly, have you ever sacrificed your work ethic, your boundaries, and your very identity just to stay in something that felt almost like love?

8

The Darkness Beneath the Mask

My heels stuck to the casino nightclub floor as I stormed toward Tyler, still in the dress I'd put on to feel beautiful for him. My face was on fire. I couldn't feel anything but rage. The music pounded so loud it rattled my teeth, but I could still hear myself screaming. It was an eruption of the truth I'd buried for too long, that was suffocated by his half-truths and carefully edited lies. It was clear now that I'd held back far more than I should have because I was smothered under his half-answers and story rewrites.

"Are you *serious* right now? Are you doing this right in *front of my face?*"

He didn't flinch. Just shifted his weight as he kept one hand planted on Rebecca's lower back. He had that same beach-day look, calm and casual as if I was the one making things weird. And Rebecca, another therapist of all things, stood there frozen, caught between guilt and curiosity, like she was waiting to see who would win.

Everyone was watching. I was the cliché, just another girlfriend losing her mind in Vegas. Our group pulled me away, whispering lines I'd heard before: "He's not doing anything wrong." "You're overreacting."

Tyler stayed with Rebecca and our other friends. He didn't come back to the hotel that night.

When Tyler finally appeared the next morning back at the hotel, he laughed like we were swapping party stories and dropped onto the bed like a frat boy after a tailgate.

"You won't believe this," he said. "An escort came up to me and tried to proposition me in the bathroom."

Of course he had a story. He always had a story. It was Florida all over again. No shame, no second thought. Just that look. I was in the Twilight Zone... again!

If you'd asked me three weeks earlier, I would've told you we were on the mend. On the drive to Easter dinner with his parents, he reached over, took my hand, and said, "I'm going to marry you. I am so in love with you." It was a much-needed flash of the man I fell in love with. But Vegas didn't come out of nowhere. The signs had been piling up for months.

Tyler began traveling more for his job as a commercial architect. I was picking up therapy clients again to pay off the farmhouse renovations that were draining us both. We weren't side-by-side anymore like we were during COVID. He had space. And he took it. While I was easing off alcohol, he was drinking more and staying out later. I'd get calls at midnight or later.

"Can you come get me?" he'd slur. "I'm at the bar up the street, I think?"

I'd drag myself out of bed, drive across town, and find him standing outside some bar like a teenager waiting to be picked up. Sometimes he'd either talk the whole ride home or pass out. In the morning, he'd act surprised.

"How did I get home? Did I call you?"

Again, I'd feel crazy. *Am I the only one living in this Twilight Zone?* Then every confrontation would begin to feel like a mirror maze. I'd walk in feeling clear, and leave wondering if I was crazy.

Meanwhile, the farmhouse renovations were not getting done. Tyler would start one project, then another, then another, and finish none of them. I'd seen this pattern before, man-boys who came on strong with big gestures and lofty plans. They'd pour themselves into something for a week, a month, a season. Just as long as it was fun. But the minute the spark wore off or someone held them accountable, it all dried up. Bring it up later, and suddenly you're the nag.

The fireplace, cabinets, and tiles sat half-installed, then left forgotten. Our living room looked like a supply yard. And I was the one paying for all of it. If I brought up hiring help, he'd roll his eyes. "Why pay someone when I can do it?" But he wasn't doing it. He instead just called it "progress." I didn't have a name for it back then, but looking back, *renovation purgatory* fits.

But it wasn't just the house. It was the pattern. The slow drip of disrespect and aloofness. One moment from that summer still haunts me. It was a moment that I brushed off back then, even though it was a sign that I couldn't name it.

His parents were hosting a pool party, and everyone was drinking. At one point, Tyler held up his empty red solo cup and flung it toward me, hitting my leg.

"Go get me another drink, woman," he said.

His mom laughed because Tyler could do no wrong. Tyler smirked, clearly pleased with himself. But I felt belittled and embarrassed. Later, when I told him how it landed, he brushed me off. "You're being emotional," he said. "It was a joke." That was always his fallback. The dismissive grin. The casual dismissal. "Relax, babe. You're being extra."

Things started to feel "off" and I had this perpetual feeling of uneasiness in my gut. A month after that Easter car ride, and a month before Vegas, something happened that didn't look like much at the time. So much so that it could've passed for innocent. But something in me registered it, quietly noted it, tucked it away for later, and then clocked it again. The same situation would explode under strobe lights in Vegas.

We had people over one night. Bourbon, music, and a few friends. One of them was Ava, a friend of a friend. She was loud, cute, and a little awkward.

I went to bed around midnight, but everyone else stayed up, including Tyler. When I woke a few hours later, the house was quiet, and Tyler wasn't next to me.

I walked over to the home bar room and saw that the light was still on, and that Tyler and Ava were sitting close, still drinking.

"She was too drunk to drive," he said. "We're just listening to music," he slurred.

I was irritated and stern, "Wrap it up now," I said. This was not a suggestion. It was a demand. "Ava, you can crash on the couch." She didn't argue. But as she stood, I noticed her boots were on, but untied, and the laces were dragging like she had been rushed.

Eventually, Tyler came to bed, and Ava disappeared. When I got up again at dawn, she was asleep in her car.

The image of those untied laces lodged in my brain and my gut. I didn't know why. It was small, but it kept circling back. Like she was rushed to take them off and got interrupted, or she was rushed to put them back on. Either way, it was odd. Later, I cautiously brought it up to Tyler.

He laughed. "Ava's not even my type. You're being paranoid."

"I didn't say you did anything," I said.

"Do you not trust me? We've built a life together, so why would I do anything to jeopardize that? Then why mention it? You're being ridiculous."

He spun it around so fast that by the end of the conversation, I was the one apologizing. He was a master justifier. For what, I still don't know.

Three weeks later, I was screaming in a nightclub while he flirted with someone else. Vegas wasn't the beginning of the end. It was the moment I stopped pretending everything was okay.

The mask hadn't slipped. It had shattered.

WHEN THE MASK STARTS TO ROT

By the time I lost my composure in Vegas, I'd been gaslit, guilted, and breadcrumbed for months. I wasn't reacting to one night of flirting. I was reacting to the slow, methodical unraveling of everything I thought I knew.

This is the part no one talks about. The moment when the mask doesn't just slip but starts to rot and peel. The man you loved doesn't disappear overnight. He mutates. He mocks your boundaries. He tests your limits. He hands you a version of himself so wildly misaligned with what came before that your brain short-circuits.

The solo cup.

The weight digs.

The new fascination with porn.

The longer work trips.

The new female work associate.

The untied boots.

The unfinished projects.

The night I'd hauled myself out of bed at 2 a.m., to find him leaning against some bar wall, slurring apologies, and then woke up to a man who acted like none of it had ever happened. This wasn't subtle. This wasn't covert. This was the Devalue and Discard Phase Sandra L. Brown warned about. It's the predictable moment when low-conscience individuals start to check out, right around the time real effort is required.

It was the same with future plans. Start big, make promises, then disappear the second follow-through is needed. I didn't yet have Sandra L. Brown's research to hold onto, the validation that would later make me feel sane again. I thought we were just in a hard stretch, something we'd work through, like healthy couples do.

I see it now. My body was sounding the alarms. But every time I tried to make sense of it, Tyler spun the story so fast I couldn't find the thread.

"You're overreacting."

"You're imagining things."

"You're sensitive."

"You're being crazy."

And eventually, I believed him. That's the cost of chronic gaslighting or what Dr. Jennifer Freyd calls Betrayal Blindness. Your body knows something's wrong, but your brain won't let you look at it head-on. That's because betrayal trauma doesn't land like a slap.

It leaks in through the cracks until you're drenched. Jennifer Freyd's research shows that when someone we depend on for safety violates our trust, the brain responds as if we're in danger. It doesn't register as simple heartbreak; it instead activates our threat response. The limbic system lights up, the memory center floods, and you start replaying everything, looking for clues you missed.

Was he like this during COVID, and I ignored it?

Was the marriage talk a lie?

Did I imagine the version of him I fell for?

Am I the one who's broken?

They were symptoms. And I had them all: anxiety, hypervigilance, and unease. Overall, a body that wouldn't settle and a mind that couldn't sort fact from fiction. I questioned my memory of events as a result.

When Tyler humiliated me at that pool party, my body flushed with embarrassment. When I found him alone with Ava at 3 a.m., my stomach clenched. When he called me for rides in the middle of the night and then forgot what happened the next day, my head pounded with confusion. Those physical sensations were warning signals from a nervous system screaming: *Something is wrong!* But I'd been conditioned to doubt myself, to second-guess my perceptions, and to do my best Taylor Swift impression: "It's me, hi, I'm the problem, it's me."

My background as a therapist didn't make me immune. If anything, it made me more invested. I wanted to understand. To contextualize. To fix. To problem-solve. That's where my Super Traits became my downfall. My loyalty kept me there long after the evidence said run. My empathy had me making excuses for his cruelty. My conscientiousness turned me into the household manager while he played. My responsibility had me working overtime to fund a life he was systematically dismantling. Tyler had turned the traits that serve me so well everywhere else into liabilities. My empathy became compliance. My loyalty became my silence. And my sense of duty kept me stuck.

This bears repeating: That's how the pattern works between strong, capable women and disordered men. The Dark Tetrad men go for women with Super Traits because the men do not possess them, and their darkness craves our glow.

Ultimately, the deeper you get, the more blinded you become to what's normal, and the harder it becomes to leave.

I'd loaned him ten grand.

Put his name on the land I bought.

Poured thousands into renovations on a shared asset

Told everyone we were building a life together.

I couldn't believe it! I'd emotionally cosigned a man who was humiliating me in front of my friends.

That's not love. That's sunk cost.

It's no wonder behavioral economists call this the Sunk Cost Fallacy, the tendency to keep investing in something that isn't working because you've already put so much into it. Research from the University of Toronto confirms what feels intuitively painful: The thought of wasting all that investment often feels worse than continuing to suffer.

And Tyler knew exactly how to play this. Each time I got close to walking away, he'd drop just enough affection, just enough future talk, and just enough charm to reset the cycle. The marriage conversation right before Vegas was a classic breadcrumbing, dropping tiny morsels of what I craved most to keep me hooked. And I'd invested so much time and energy.

What makes this dynamic so toxic is the cognitive dissonance, that maddening gap between what I knew intellectually and what I felt emotionally. My brain couldn't reconcile the man who was attentive during COVID with the man who threw a cup at me and demanded a drink. Or the man who talked about marriage with the man who stayed out all night, flirting with another woman. So, my brain did what brains do when faced with opposing truths. It tried to resolve the dissonance.

Either he wasn't that bad, and I was overreacting (which made me question my sanity)...

Or he was exactly that bad, and I had been fooled (which made me question my decision-making).

Either way, I lost. Either way, I felt confused, uncertain of my sanity, and broken.

That's the true insidious genius of the devaluation game. He doesn't need to lie or cheat every night to destroy you. All he has to do is plant enough self-doubt that you stop trusting your perception of reality. Because once you admit the truth, you have to face everything that came before it. You have to reckon with the version of yourself who stayed, who hoped, and who handed over pieces of her life to someone who didn't deserve them.

For a long time, I was that person, until the reckoning thankfully happened.

It's the beginning of freedom.

But no doubt. It's a painful process to go through.

THE BODY'S QUIET REBELLION

I didn't leave after Vegas. I wish I had. I wish I could say that was the moment I slammed the door and never looked back. But it wasn't.

And if you're still here, still circling this same decision, I need you to hear this: That doesn't make you weak. That doesn't make you blind. It means your nervous system is doing exactly what it's wired to do when the person you love becomes the person who harms you. It means your mind and your body are in conflict, and your body is trying to get your attention, so you have to scream through the noise.

The unraveling didn't happen with a single blow. It happened in a series of internal revolts. Like tiny paper cuts over four years. Tiny rebellions incited by my intuition.

It began with a flush of shame because I knew something was off, but couldn't figure it out. Then sleepless nights, headaches, anxiety, and intrusive thoughts out of nowhere. But that's how I started to know. Before I had the words, before I had hard proof, my body knew.

When he brushed off my concerns with that same dead-eyed indifference, my chest tightened. These weren't random symptoms. I've felt these before with my first psychopathic boyfriend. But I was still looking for answers. I was still looking for the *"Why is he acting this way?"* instead of *"This is how he is acting. Period."* Nonetheless, these were alarms.

Bessel van der Kolk calls it somatic memory, the body keeping score. And mine had been racking up a list that couldn't be gaslit away. Every pang, every flush, every clench was the nervous system sounding the alarm before my brain could catch up. Unfortunately, I didn't trust my feelings yet.

And then there were the images I couldn't shake. Her boots. The laces. The way he said, "You're being paranoid" with that half-smile. Those moments started to change shape, from confusion to clarity, and from coincidence to pattern. I began to pull back—first in my mind—as I worked to shift the power imbalance in my favor. I argued less, watched more. I stopped trying to get him to see me, and I started seeing him instead.

My body led the way. When he walked into a room and I tensed, I took note. When I waited for the next dig, the next disappearance, I stopped pretending I didn't see it coming. This wasn't anxiety. It was recognition.

That's the beginning of disentanglement. When you stop performing in the relationship and start observing it. When you stop explaining yourself and start listening to the data. When you respond from grounded wisdom instead of reacting from old habits, everything starts to come into focus.

You don't need a full-blown revelation. You need a quiet shift. A decision that starts in your skin before it ever reaches your voice. This is what healing looks like at first. You're still in the house, but no longer in the story. You're still in the relationship, but no longer rewriting it.

You don't *have* to leave today.

But you can start listening. Logging. Knowing.

And once you know, you can't unknow.

That's when the spell breaks.

That's when you begin to return to yourself.

That's when leaving starts to feel less like a cliff and more like a path. A hard path, yes. But, one you can walk.

And each step is one step closer to yourself.

THE ECHO CHAMBER

I sat on the couch reading my old journal entries. My whole life was scribbled on delicate paper in leatherbound journals. There were decades of raw emotions about past boyfriends scrawled across the pages. The same tight feeling arose in my chest. I read the pages line by line like I was disarming a bomb. I was on the edge of each page, hoping they might hold a clue I missed the first time. My breathing was shallow. My stomach, a hard knot.

I didn't need a therapist to tell me what I was doing. I was looking for the pattern. And there it was:

The bad boy with the motorcycle who held a gun to my head when I tried to leave.

The polished engineer who vanished for days, then reappeared with gifts and excuses.

The charming architect whose warmth evaporated the moment I needed accountability from him.

Three different men. Three different costumes. But beneath every mask, the same playbook. The telltale sign? Escalating behavior and a blatant disregard for me—and for us. Each one zeroing in on the same qualities, targeting the same parts of me, and using what was best in me as a weapon.

Tyler pinning me down in the hotel, calling it "just playing," lit up the same gut-deep nausea I'd felt with Brian's 9MM pistol pressed to my temple. Tyler's vanishing acts echoed Mark's disappearances, and the same hollow ache in my chest, the same effort to act unbothered. Every twisted apology. Every deflection. The way they turned my concern into proof of my instability and irrationality. It was the same playbook, just a different game.

I thought about the early stages: the whirlwind connection, the curated vulnerability that made me feel chosen. The mirroring. The boundary pushing disguised as intimacy. The friends I drifted from, because "they didn't get it." The long stretches of neglect, interrupted by flurries of affection, just enough to keep me hooked. Once it all clicked, there was no unseeing it. It was deliberate!

I learned how repeated betrayal rewires the nervous system. How intensity starts to feel like intimacy. How anxiety gets misread as attraction. My betrayal trauma coach had recommended the work of Sandra L. Brown, whose research didn't just explain the trauma, but named the pattern. Named what I had been searching for for years. The missing puzzle piece. It was there, clear as day. I was a magnet. Or more specifically, my Super Traits were the magnet. Women like me, like you, with the Super Traits, are hunted for our loyalty, empathy, and strength. It was all there, in black and white. Cue the dramatic music! This was it! This was the missing piece!

It all made sense. My body wasn't broken. It had been trained. My story wasn't a fluke. It was a case study. That made sense now.

But that knowledge hit me like grief. It also cracked something open. I started to listen to my body differently. The tightness in my chest was a memory, not oversensitivity. The instinct to shrink when someone made a joke at my expense wasn't insecurity; it was a signal. The dread before the phone call and the drop in my stomach when the tone shifted were all wisdom I'd spent years overriding. My Super Traits, once used against me, became my compass.

My loyalty turned inward. My conscientiousness evolved into discernment. My empathy began to include myself. My agreeableness made space for boundaries.

These days, it usually happens on early dates. I see now how their stories don't quite match, the jokes come with a sting, or they want too much too soon. I can spot them quickly now, and I want to teach other women like you how to do the same.

I've figured the pattern out. I can feel it. I recognize the banal opening notes and I keep it moving. I don't push it down anymore. I don't rationalize. I finish my coffee—no more bourbon. I leave. No explanations needed! In the silence that follows, my body doesn't brace for the next blow. My chest softens. My jaw unclenches. That's how I know I'm not trying to convince myself anymore. I'm following myself. I am guarding my glow and protecting my light in the darkness.

My Super Traits haven't gone anywhere. They've recalibrated. My sensitivity is my filter. My body, my compass. My loyalty is no longer a leash.

That's because I now know when I am experiencing cognitive dissonance, and I don't second-guess myself and mistake the ache as a reason to stay.

Now it's the signal to go.

REAL TALK: YOUR BODY KEEPS RECEIPTS

Your body has been tracking the truth the whole time. The knots in your stomach before he walks into the room. The headache after he "explains" why you misunderstood him. The tightness you feel in your chest when your phone lights up when he texts. The weight behind your eyes when you're getting dressed to see him, and something in you resists. These weren't mood swings or stress. I used to explain mine away. *Maybe I'm hormonal. Maybe I'm anxious. Maybe I'm too sensitive.* Meanwhile, my nervous system was flaring like a car alarm. They were warnings I'd spent years learning to silence.

Here's the truth I wish I'd learned earlier: The body remembers what the heart wants to forget. And the more you honor those signals, the sooner they become your filter. Your compass. Your north star.

You don't need a spreadsheet or a smoking gun. You just need to start believing in yourself the first time. As you learn to recognize your body's signals, you'll respond with clarity and confidence. Then the next time something feels off, your body will speak first. And this time, you'll know What I Think It Means.

This is how we stop repeating the cycle.

We stop explaining it away.

We start listening.

Because your body doesn't lie.

 # LET'S REFLECT

I told myself, "I'm just stressed."

But what I was feeling wasn't stress, it was my body sounding the alarm. The knots in my stomach, the tightness in my chest, the headache that showed up after every "misunderstanding." These weren't random symptoms. They were data.

And let's be real: I wanted to believe the story my heart was telling more than the one my body was living.

That's how women wired for connection can talk themselves out of their own truth.

Super Traits He Targeted:

- High tolerance for discomfort

- Belief in redemption

- Self-reflection that turned into self-blame

Red Flags My Body Registered First:

- Physical tension or anxiety before seeing him

- Fatigue or headaches after conversations

 ## JOURNAL COACHING MOMENT

Find a quiet space, take a deep breath, and let yourself reflect honestly, without judgment or pressure. This is your space to explore, not to be perfect.

Think of a time when your body reacted before your brain had evidence. What was the sensation—tightness, nausea, fatigue, shallow breathing?

Do your last few dates or relationships have similarities? Look for patterns. List the facts, situation, and physical and emotional response.

What story did you tell yourself at the time to explain it away?

Looking back now, what was your body trying to communicate?

How might your choices have shifted if you had trusted that first signal?

For the next week, track your physical responses in all interactions—not just romantic ones. Which sensations repeat? Which people or situations trigger them?

9

The Collapse

JOURNAL ENTRY
I wanted to see what I wanted to see,
and I chose to see the "good." He
wasn't a loving individual with an evil
twin. He was the evil twin who happened
to have good moments.

I couldn't shake the image of those untied boots.

It had been months since that night, but the visual kept surfacing of Ava's boots, loosely laced and dragging across the floor at 3 a.m. Was she taking them off when I walked in? Or rushing to tie them up again after? Either way, something about it wouldn't leave me. My gut kept circling back to that moment. I didn't know what I was looking for, but my body did.

Late July came with its heaviness. I flew to Michigan for a work trip, right around what would've been my mom's birthday. I'd expected grief to be the hardest part of that week, but Tyler had other plans.

The day I left, he mentioned some acting gig out of nowhere. "It's this background extra thing. I'll probably be in the crowd of a bar scene or something," he said, pacing with sudden energy that didn't match the moment. I remember thinking it felt off. Where did this even come from? It was like I was looking at a different person altogether. But by then, I had no energy to deal with his shenanigans so I dismissed it.

When I got home a few days later, he was already heading out. And I couldn't shake it anymore. That uneasy pull in my gut wouldn't let go. That's when I saw his work phone, face-down on the desk, its silence daring me to flip it over. My breath halted as my mind pulled me back to that night at our favorite Mexican place when I squinted at the Tinder flame on his screen while he laughed it off. Now, with sweaty palms, I flipped his phone over and swiped through screens. And there they were, mocking me: Adult Friend Finder and Ashley Madison. Two little logos that slammed into my heart like bullets, violently confirming the nightmare I'd refused to believe.

With trembling fingers, I clicked "Inbox," exposing the faces of all the strangers he'd been texting while I was leading corporate meetings and financing our lifestyle. There were photos and meetups. There were messages such as, "I like submissive" and "I want to taste you." Full-blown conversations with strangers about what he wanted, what he would do to them, and what they could do for him. This wasn't curiosity. This wasn't boredom. This was premeditated, serial betrayal.

With breath caught in my throat I proceeded to call his personal phone. He answered with a curt, detached "Hey, what's up?" Like I'd interrupted him.

"What is going on, Tyler?"

"What?"

"Adult Friend Finder? Ashley Madison? Are you kidding me?"

His voice went cold, annoyed. "You went through my phone? That's such an invasion of privacy."

I didn't even wait for an explanation. I yelled, demanding he turn the car around and come back. When he finally swung into our driveway, I was there waiting, trembling with a white-hot fury I'd never known. Before he could step out of his car, I kicked the first thing I saw at him: an empty Amazon box. My voice cracked as I hurled every insult I could summon.

"Does four years mean nothing to you? Who *are* you? I don't even know you right now!"

Tyler didn't even flinch. His face remained completely blank, cold, and eerily detached.

For a flash of a second, I saw my first boyfriend's face, the one who punched me in the face after I confronted him about cheating. That same empty gaze. The same hint of a smirk that said, "You shouldn't have done that." Both of them watched me unravel while they felt nothing. That look still haunts me to this day.

Later that night, I wrote in my journal:

I found out on Thursday that Tyler was on Adult Friend Finder, Ashley Madison, and several other sites trying to find hookups. I'm devastated, sad, angry, hurt, and numb. I fear I'm always going to be alone. I've overcome so much.

His explanation, when he finally gave one, made my skin crawl.

"I was just seeing if I still had it. If other women find me desirable."

Narcissistic Supply. The term floated up from my clinical training. He needed validation from outside sources because he felt empty inside. This wasn't impulse or confusion. It was fuel for the gaping hole in his chest. He didn't care what it cost me. He never had.

With my adrenaline now surging, I flung clothes and essentials into the Jeep I'd financed myself, slammed the door, and tore down the interstate toward Chattanooga to crash with my bestie. While I was there, raw and reeling, Tyler staged a "support party" for himself at our shared home in Georgia. His friends gathered round his pouting act, murmured sympathy, and offered tissues for his wounded pride. My phone buzzed nonstop: "Tyler's so sad you left... he's been sulking all night."

Playing the victim. Gathering allies. Tyler was already rewriting the story.

••

The days stretched longer, but the fog inside me stayed thick. I went through the motions—worked, ate, slept—but nothing settled. Part of me still clung to the story I'd built in my head: maybe this was our rock bottom. Maybe he would finally see the damage he'd caused and be ready to change.

And I wasn't the only one who held onto that hope. His family called constantly, reassuring me that he was brokenhearted, that he loved me, that this was a mistake. Friends reached out, telling me how devastated he was that I'd left, and how he couldn't eat or sleep without me. The pressure was everywhere: "He knows he messed up." "He just needs another chance." "Don't throw it all away."

Meanwhile, Tyler played his part perfectly. "I wasn't looking for anything serious," he said over and over. "I made a terrible mistake." Then he said what he knew I wanted to hear, that he was ready to do the work, and he believed our love was worth fighting for.

This all kept me bargaining with a fantasy. I was still trying to hold on to the dream with the shared home, family, and friends. There was just so much to untangle. So, I came home to figure out next steps. It was like I'd locked the door behind me, but the key was still in my pocket. And for a little while, things calmed down again.

We were sleeping in separate rooms now, but we were talking, really talking, more than we had in months. Tyler seemed like a changed man. He came across as humbled, contrite. He was in therapy. I was in therapy. We were "dating" again, carefully, like trying to rebuild a house after a fire.

While part of me stayed guarded, waiting for the next match to drop. Another part, the one that had survived so much already, started to believe maybe he'd finally woken up and realized what he almost lost. Maybe the worst had passed. Seeing how hindsight is sharp and unforgiving, I ultimately silenced my instincts. I knew what I *should* have done. But I didn't do it.

Not because I didn't know. But because the truth required action, and I wasn't ready to take. I was entangled. Emotionally, financially, logistically. I kept weighing the cost of leaving against the comfort of staying. And in that mental tug-of-war, denial felt easier than disruption. And honestly I was flat out exhausted.

A month later, I was still trying to make sense of everything, still trying to figure out if anything we'd built was real and if he was really trying to heal our relationship. Then my phone lit up at 3 a.m. It was a text from Ava:

Hey, you know your boyfriend got another woman pregnant. He paid for her abortion and raised hell when he thought she didn't go through with it. Just letting you know.

THE PSYCHOPATH MANIFESTO

I stared at the message, my mind spinning through possibilities. Wrong number? Mistaken identity? She must have meant someone else.

His chest rose and fell beside me, steady and undisturbed. I set the phone back down. *Probably a drunk text.* I'd deal with it in the morning.

When I woke up, I read it again. I had to know.

"Hey, I got this strange text from Ava last night," I said casually over coffee, like I was asking about the weather. "It said something about a pregnancy."

He didn't blink. No confusion. No denial. No horror or outrage. Cool as a cucumber. Then he exhaled and said, "I need to tell you something."

That sentence punched a hole through my chest.

He spoke coolly and deliberately while I disappeared inside myself. He told me that he had made out with Ava. That maybe more happened, but he was too drunk to remember. That she'd said she was pregnant. That she'd asked for money. And finally, that she was "crazy."

Tyler kept talking, but my mind blurred at the edges, like it was trying not to take any more in. I stumbled to the bathroom, washed my face through burning tears, all the while trying to steady myself for the client presentation I was supposed to give in two hours. Then tunnel vision set in, my face flushed hot, and my breath locked somewhere between my chest and throat. I was having a full-blown panic attack. Then I somehow reapplied my makeup, straightened my blazer, and left for work to stand in front of a room full of executives as if my life hadn't just been blown to pieces. Over-functioning much?

My world was crumbling underneath my heels, but there I was, smiling, nodding, performing. Because that's what women like us do. We show up. We hold it together. Until we can't.

But by the time I got home, rage had crystallized into something sharper. Something colder. Clarity.

"Tell me everything," I said, sitting across from him. "Every woman. Every lie. I want to know exactly who I've been living with."

Tyler's eyes locked eyes with mine. He exhibited no anxiety, no nervousness. Of course, he didn't. Research shows that Dark Tetrad individuals show significant impairments in empathy and virtually no anxiety response. They don't feel shame the way normal people do. They run assessments instead. I'd seen that look before. He wasn't sifting through guilt. He was running algorithms. Plotting the next move. But after five hours of interrogation, Tyler cracked.

He broke into sobs, blaming it all on a sex addiction. That was his excuse.

The tears came easily, like he'd practiced for the role. Maybe those acting classes were finally paying off! Crocodile tears, perfectly queued. But my clinical brain wasn't buying it. I know what addiction looks like. This wasn't it. Dr. Omar Minwalla calls it the Secret Sexual Basement, a compartmentalized world of hidden sexual, romantic, and emotional deception. It's not a few isolated slip-ups, but an entire double life deliberately walled off from the primary relationship. Minwalla calls it Deceptive, Compartmentalized Sexual-Relational Reality (DCSR), and he's right: it's not impulsivity. It's psychological abuse. A pattern of sustained manipulation that systematically dismantles the partner's reality.

Ava wasn't some one-off drunken mistake. As it turned out, he told me she was one of four women he'd slept with that year alone. His "work trips" to Phoenix were detours to Vegas to take women on dates. The "work emergency" that kept him from flying home was another woman entirely.

And then there was the lotion. He once gave me a scenting lotion, told me it reminded him of me. Months later, I found out it was one of his other women's signature scents. Diabolical.

"Did you use protection?" I asked.

A pause.

"Not always."

My stomach lurched. My health. My future. My body. All treated like collateral damage in his private pursuit of stimulation.

"He was calm as a cucumber," I told my therapist later. "And that told me everything I needed to know."

This wasn't a relationship breakdown. This wasn't a man in crisis. This was a predator who'd been caught, calculating his best play.

I scheduled STD testing for the next morning. He'd been living a double life, and I'd been treating it like a relationship rough patch. What I was staring at wasn't just a string of betrayals. It was a pattern I'd never been taught to recognize, an intricate system of manipulation designed to satisfy his needs while dismantling my reality.

••

About three weeks after Ava's text, while staying at his parents' house, Tyler sent me an email. The subject line read "Please Read This." A twelve-page letter was attached. What landed in my inbox that day became what I now call the "Psychopath Manifesto," a document so saturated with manipulation techniques it could have been pulled from a clinical study.

The deflection started immediately:

"What if I had a gambling addiction and put us in mega debt and had to get help for it? Would you leave me? What if I was an

alcoholic and had to go to rehab? Would you leave me?"

He was trying to play on my loyalty, twisting my instinct to leave into a character flaw. My boundaries were heartless, he said. My self-preservation was cold. Translation: You're cruel for having limits.

"Love is about the good and the bad," he continued, "fighting for a relationship when it seems impossible, supporting your partner when they make a mistake, and being there when they need you."

Another desperate bid to rewrite the script. Suddenly, my expectation of fidelity was unreasonable. My desire for honesty was rigid. This manifesto was a sick attempt to manipulate me into feeling I was the one who needed to prove my devotion. Translation: If you loved me, you'd tolerate betrayal. False contrition came next, dressed in therapy-speak.

"Maybe my personality traits do align with a psychopath, but I don't believe I am one. And even still, they can also get help and recover."

He named his pathology, then minimized it in the next breath. The acknowledgment of his character defect melted immediately into the promise of change, a promise I'd heard in different forms for months. Translation: Maybe I fit the profile, but you owe me another chance.

"Constance, I love you, and I'm sorry I hurt you. But I'm not prepared to let you go. We have way too much love and an amazing life ahead of us. I'm not going to let you walk away like this. Please try

to find it in your heart to forgive me and give me a second chance."

More love bombing. Future faking. I'd heard it all before. Translation: Your loyalty should matter more than your sanity.

And notice the language: "I'm not prepared to let you go." "I'm not going to let you walk away." "Please don't abandon us."

As if my leaving was an action being done *to* him. As if my autonomy required his permission. Translation: My choices don't matter. Only your loyalty does. Because that's the core of disordered manipulation: everything is measured by how it affects them.

Then came one of the most shameless lines in the entire letter:

"I joined Adult Friend Finder. It really started with curiosity more than anything... I could engage in the attempt of hooking up, without cheating. In a way, I was feeding the urge, but also safeguarding us."

Chivalry was not dead! He cheated *for us*. My pain was collateral damage in his self-healing journey. It would've been textbook rationalization if it hadn't been so pathetic. Translation: I only hurt you to protect you.

But the manifesto didn't stop there. It was flooded with future promises:

"I will earn your trust back. You can set the terms—I'll do anything... I would rather sacrifice any amount of freedom than lose you."

The same promises I'd heard in the early days:

"You are all the things. Everything I could ever want in a partner and a wife... You're emotionally intelligent, trained to handle psychologically complicated individuals, and really sexy."

Words crafted perfectly for someone with Super Traits. The perfect bait for my loyalty, my empathy, and my hope. But he didn't stop there. More future faking:

"I will put you first. I will love you the way you deserve. I will be truthful. I will be vulnerable. I will be open."

Every "I will" is a reaction to a failure already committed. Every promise is a breadcrumb meant to lure me back. Translation: Ignore what I've done. Believe what I'm promising.

If you're loyal, hopeful, someone who believes love can heal, you know these words too well. But this time, when I read his words, something shifted. I recognized that it was the same script, recycled and predictable. They were new words, same manipulation. For the first time, I didn't read them as a lover. I read them as a clinician. As a result, the patterns snapped into focus, and the manipulation stood naked.

I'd spent years believing people could heal with enough love and support. That transgressions could be worked through and that relationships could be rebuilt when two people were willing. But these scripts don't apply in a relationship with a Dark Tetrad individual.

Tyler's letter forced a different truth into view. Dark Tetrads don't stumble. They calculate. Tyler knew exactly which promises to make, which triggers to press, which emotions to counterfeit. But it was too little, too late.

THE CLINICAL AWAKENING

"We are warned about food and environmental contaminants, the public-health risks of not using condoms, how to protect ourselves from rape or attack. Why not be warned of the safety risks related to a partner with little or no empathy, no conscience?"

I didn't know research like Sandra L. Brown's existed until the damage had already been done. No one had taught me to watch for these patterns. Not in graduate school, not in training, not in supervision, and certainly not in the lessons I grew up with. Not from teachers. Not from parents. Not from a culture that celebrates the triumph of staying, but rarely honors the strength it takes to leave.

Even our emergency couples therapist, who showed up to our $1,500-intensive session hungover from a concert the night before, told me Tyler had empathy. "He cried about the dog," he said. "He's remorseful."

The dog. Not me. The freaking dog. For a split second, I wanted to flip the conference table. Instead, I sat perfectly still, feeling every illusion about healing as they cracked at the edges.

When I finally found Brown's work, it landed like a missing piece of my own story, one I suspect many women reading this have been waiting to find as well. My body had recognized what my formal education never named. But I had to lose almost everything to realize that, when it comes to the Dark Tetrad, the rules are different.

Tyler didn't stumble into hurting me. He moved through the world, taking what he wanted, without weighing the cost to anyone else. My empathy, loyalty, and willingness to believe make me powerful in healthy relationships. He turned these same traits into levers to manipulate me. His friends texted me about how "broken up" he was. His parents defended him: "She's crazy, he's a good guy who's been through a lot." His family and friends reinforced the cultural fairytale: the beast becoming the prince, the villain finding redemption, and the wounded boy healing through the power of love. But the clinical research is brutally clear. Personality disorders tied to the Dark Tetrad are fundamentally resistant to change.

Personality psychologist Delroy L. Paulhus points to low honesty-humility as the defining commonality across narcissism, Machiavellianism, psychopathy, and sadism. These individuals do not value sincerity, fairness, or remorse. They lie, exploit, and manipulate because deep down, they don't recognize others as fully real or equal.

The research of another personality psychologist, Nathan W. Hudson, points to the same conclusion: Therapy is not a solution when the core operating system is designed to exploit. Change requires discomfort. It requires admitting vulnerability. By definition, dark personalities refuse both. My betrayal trauma coach said it best: "These types have been training for this their whole lives. It's like the Olympics of learned empathy."

Tyler's brag, "I'm a chameleon. I can fit in anywhere," wasn't the tell of a quirky strength. It was a confession. Dark Tetrad individuals shift personas to suit the audience. Opportunism replaces loyalty. Super Traits like empathy and conscientiousness are alien to them. They are, in fact, the very qualities they seek out, because they make exploitation easier and consequences less likely.

I looked around our half-renovated house, and at all the grand plans that were abandoned, and projects that were started, then forgotten the moment they required actual effort. They were the literal manifestation of Tyler's approach to everything: Make big promises, create exciting beginnings, then disappear when carrying out becomes necessary. There was the life he showed me, and the basement full of everything he didn't.

Tyler was such a textbook profile that he literally fit this description by Paul Hokemeyer: "The personality traits that make up a Dark Tetrad are deeply ingrained in their psyche and highly resistant to any sort of challenge that would manifest a change."

His advice? "The best strategy is to move away from them as quickly as possible.... No contact."

Tyler wasn't confused. He wasn't broken in a way that could be healed by love, insight, or patience. He was operating according to design. And accepting this didn't happen in my head. It happened in my body. The cognitive dissonance cracked open. The fog that once kept me stuck finally lifted, and I could see the pattern in full.

The old hooks lost their grip. The cycles of affection and abandonment that once pulled me back couldn't touch me anymore. I stopped second-guessing what I saw. I stopped diluting what I felt, and the pain stripped itself bare.

What's more, I wasn't weeping for him anymore. I was instead fighting for the parts of myself he thought he could bury.

Healing wasn't about rebuilding the relationship. It was about deconstructing every false narrative that had kept me tethered. I'd previously thought of healing as reconstruction, rebuilding what was broken. Now I recognized healing meant dismantling the beliefs, expectations, and hopes that kept me bound to someone incapable of genuine attachment. For so long, I'd hoped Tyler would change. I now understood the most profound change had occurred within me. I now could recognize the pattern, I could name the manipulation, and I could finally trust my perceptions.

The damage from relationships with Dark Tetrad men runs deeper than heartbreak. Researchers like Sandra L. Brown have shown what survivors know firsthand: Many of us walk away carrying clinical Post-Traumatic Stress Disorder (PTSD). That's because it severs your reality. It dismantles your ability to trust what you see, what you feel, and what you know. It rewires your nervous system until confusion feels like love and anxiety feels like connection. I was one of them. I left the relationship a shell of myself, carrying the weight of that diagnosis.

We use all these shiny words like trauma bonds, betrayal trauma, and cognitive dissonance. But at the heart of it, the equation is simple: People wired like this—psychopaths, narcissists, Machiavellians, sadists—don't just hurt you once and move on. They drain you until there's nothing left. Then they blame you for bleeding.

Tyler was never coming back. Because the Tyler I thought I loved never existed.

And once you see the pattern, you will never unsee it.

You don't wait for them to heal. You heal yourself.

And you get out.

THE THINGS YOU DON'T GET BACK

I walked into my attorney's office three months after leaving Tyler, holding a folder stuffed with bank statements, emails, and screenshots.

"I didn't think I'd end up here," I said.

She didn't look up. "Nobody does. Nobody warns you what staying costs until you've already paid too much."

What had staying cost me? What did it keep costing, long after he was gone? I've lost twenty years to disordered relationships. Not all at once. Slowly, in pieces. Years with one man who kept me guessing, another who wore me down with emotional unavailability, and one who mirrored me just long enough to hook me to discard me. And through it all, I kept making choices that kept me there, and I am owning this.

If you're still in one of these relationships. If you're still hoping, still excusing, still rationalizing, let me tell you what's at stake. It drains you financially. Tyler alone cost me dearly in attorney fees and lost homes, thousands spent in therapy trying to salvage something designed to collapse, and a line of credit tied to the house that was draining my account every month. A house that lost value because Tyler couldn't finish a single project he started.

But money's easy to measure. It's the other stuff that's harder to name, and harder to get back. For one, your nervous system becomes a crime scene. I slept in fits. I couldn't eat, I couldn't breathe. I felt like I was bracing for impact, even in silence. Yet somehow, I still kept my career afloat while I moved cities, rebuilt my life, and held it all together while I came apart inside. Your body keeps score even when your mind refuses to. The night sweats. The phantom phone checks. The constant startled response. The tightness in your chest. The digestive issues. Pay attention to how your body feels when your person appears. The subtle tensing. The shallow breathing. The way your thoughts scatter slightly to reorganize around their moods, their needs, and their expectations. Your body has the receipts your mind has shredded.

But it still seeped into my work. I'd sit through meetings with red eyes, half-listening, half-remembering what I was supposed to be doing. Deadlines slipped. Conversations blurred. That's because my mind wasn't in the office. It was back at the house, in the unanswered questions and odd behaviors. Back in the silence that rotted everything from the inside out. You lose more than time in these relationships. You lose your stability. You lose presence. You lose the part of yourself that once believed anything was possible.

You lose friends, too. You stop showing up. Stop sharing. You isolate yourself because you're ashamed.

And the question always comes: Why didn't you just leave?

As if love ever feels that clear when you're in it. As if staying too long means you deserved the explosion that followed. Like, your punishment was fair for not running fast enough.

It's easy to lay it all out neatly on the page and dissect it in hindsight. But it never feels like a sudden collapse while you're living it. It's not a waterfall. It's a slow drip, one small compromise after another stretched out over the years.

And like so many of you, we had beautiful moments. Great vacations. Laughter. It wasn't all bad. Until it was.

So, when you do leave? There's no right answer, but there are consequences if you wait too long. You'll leave a version of yourself behind. The one who laughed more. The one who trusted easily. The one who didn't have to track inconsistencies like an FBI agent with a whiteboard full of lies.

This isn't one man. This is a pattern. Brian taught me fear and violence. Mark taught me to settle for almost love. And Tyler brought it all together: the gaslighting, the dual lives, and the polished facade. That's the cost. Each relationship builds scar tissue. And each wound makes it harder to feel clearly in the next relationship. That's because the Dark Tetrad doesn't start the damage. They finish the job.

Yes, the women who leave at the first sign of gaslighting, control, or disrespect hurt. They grieve. They question. But they walk away with their core still intact.

The women who stay and convince themselves it will change, that love conquers all, and that commitment means never walking away, bleed out slowly. By the time they leave, they've lost so much that they hardly recognize themselves.

I've been both women. The second version hurts worse.

I want you to hear this with your whole chest: The longer you stay, the more it takes. The sooner you name the pattern, the more you get to keep.

"But I see the good in him." "But no one else understands how strong our connection really is." "We're working through it." I wanted to believe all of that, too. And I did, until it was too late.

Every woman whose heart I've held in therapy sessions wanted to believe it. The high-powered attorneys. The physicians. The teachers. The therapists. Women with advanced degrees and brilliant minds who fell for men who fed on exactly what made them special.

When I finally left, there were no fireworks. Only a door closing. I packed what I could, called a friend, and moved out while he was at work. I had anxiety meds, a coach, a therapist, and a thousand loose threads to tie off. But I also had something I hadn't had in years: Quiet. Stillness. Peace. Which led me to find myself again in the most ordinary ways. Like, while choosing paint colors. Or when cooking alone. And while laughing at something without checking if he thought it was funny, too.

The house I live in now is smaller, less impressive. But it's mine. No unfinished projects mock me from the corner. No secrets are buried in burner phones. I no longer rearranged my sense of reality to make a grown man's conscience make sense.

This is what clarity preserves. This is what gets to stay when you stop bleeding for someone who won't even stop lying.

Your empathy can heal people. But only if it's safe. Your loyalty can change lives. But only if it's met. Your conscientiousness can build something beautiful, but only if you're not constantly rebuilding what someone else tears down.

These gifts we carry, these Super Traits that make us targets for the Dark Tetrad, belong to *us*. They make us powerful. They connect us to others. They create beauty in the world.

But they require protection. I don't want you to hit bottom before you believe me. I don't want you to have to burn your life down just to start again.

You can walk away now and leave the wreckage behind you, where it belongs.

REAL TALK: ONCE YOU NAME IT, YOU DON'T GO BACK TO SLEEP

Once you see the pattern for what it is, the mask for what it hides, you never forget. You don't waste another year trying to find the man he pretended to be. You instead save the woman he never really knew.

If you're reading this, something inside you already knows.

Maybe you have your version of the untied boots, some small detail you can't unsee. Maybe you found the texts you weren't supposed to know about. Maybe you've been living with that constant, quiet dread, the feeling that something vital doesn't add up. Your body knows something is up before your mind can catch up.

Now, let's honor that knowing.

LET'S REFLECT

The Dark Tetrad thrives on hesitation. They bank on your loyalty outlasting your limits. They count on your empathy to keep you chained to their chaos. They rely on your conscientiousness to convince you there's always one more thing you should try.

But the uncomfortable truth is that you already know. You knew before the texts. You knew before the excuses. You knew before the dread swallowed your sleep. You don't need more proof. What you need is your permission.

So take back what's yours.

Start now. Start messy. Start scared. Start.

JOURNAL COACHING MOMENT

Find a quiet space, take a deep breath, and let yourself reflect honestly, without judgment or pressure. This is your space to explore, not to be perfect.

Part 1: Your Body's Wisdom

Write down three physical sensations you experience when your partner:

- Comes home late without explanation

- Tells you a story that doesn't quite track

- Suddenly becomes sweet after pulling away for days

Your body isn't lying to you. It's protecting you.

Part 2: The Shifting Stories

List anything that stands out:

- Conversations they forgot having

- Moments you were made to defend reality

- Stories that changed depending on the audience

- Absences that never fully made sense

Look for repetition, not explanations.

Part 3: The Emotional Math

For each category, list what you give and what you get:

- Admiration (Compliments, encouragement)

- Trust (Openness, honesty)

- Resources (Time, money, emotional labor)

- Future plans (Actual steps or vague promises)

Healthy partnerships balance. Exploitative ones drain.

Part 4: The Reality Check

Circle anything you've felt:

- I have to explain basic decency to them.

- I feel crazy even when I know I'm right.

- They lie, but somehow I end up apologizing.

- Their tears dry up fast once I forgive them.

- They show more concern for appearances than for my pain.

- When I'm upset, they act indifferent.

Three or more circled? It's not a rough patch. It's a pattern.

Part 5: The Way Out

Ask yourself:

- Has staying made things better?

- What advice would I give my best friend?

- Can I honestly imagine feeling safe here one year from today?

My Traits,
My Tools, My Turn

I wish I could tell you I've completely healed. That trust is restored 100%. That everything is all tied up in a bow.

The truth? Some days, my mind still blindsides me. Out of nowhere, it'll erupt, dragging me right back to the betrayal, to the manipulation, and to the red flags I once kept explaining away. One moment, I'm condemning him. Next, I'm condemning myself for what I missed. For what I tolerated. For what I excused.

That's because I didn't first encounter this pattern with Tyler. It was decades earlier. A different man, a different mask, but the same pathology. The same man who once pressed a gun to my temple after love bombing me into believing I was his world. That was my first introduction to what happens when adoration turns violent. And even back then, I rationalized it away. I thought I could fix it. I thought it was love.

When you survive a relationship with someone from the Dark Tetrad, you don't just lose a partner like in ordinary breakups. You lose your grasp on reality itself. Your sense of fairness collapses. Your belief in human goodness fractures. Regular breakups leave scars that fade. This leaves you fundamentally altered. Suddenly, you're aware of dangers others can't even see.

The supposedly isolated drunken mistake with Ava wasn't isolated at all. It was one skeleton in a basement overflowing with secrets and calculated deception that was far worse than I had suspected and more extensive than I could have imagined. It led me to discover that Tyler had solicited strangers for sex. He'd trolled hookup sites under fake names, arranged meetings in cities he claimed to travel to for work, and fed his addiction for attention at the cost of my safety, my sanity, and my health. He'd even signed up to be an escort, for Christ's sake. How many people were there? I'll never know. But when the mask is that polished and the basement that deep, you eventually give up trying to count.

Two weeks after I left, he moved her in. A new woman. Or maybe one he'd been courting for months. Another source of supply. She posted flowers and camping trips on social media, eerily familiar snapshots of my past replayed through an unsuspecting understudy. A couple of years after that, he got married. Just a few days ago, three years after I finally left, I got a text from a friend with a link: Tyler and his new wife had turned our old land into a wedding venue. She'd quit her day job to run it, using the exact business plan I created when we were together. The irony wasn't lost on me. This man, divorced twice by thirty, had made me feel like "the one" by calling every woman before me crazy. Now he was selling fairy tales on land I financed. But what burned wasn't the irony that he, of all people, would sell people a happily-ever-after. No, it was watching him hijack my dream, repackage it, and run the same cycle: acquire, exploit, discard, and repeat.

Like I said, there are days when this injustice still makes my blood boil. But even in those moments, I'm not that shattered woman anymore. I've moved beyond heartbreak to clarity. When I left, I knew what mattered most was defending what I'd let undeserving men abuse. The legal battle could wait. The house could wait. I had to defend myself. My nervous system, my finances, my future. And most importantly, my Super Traits.

Your agreeableness, the warm, open nature once used against you, can now help you hold your pain with the same compassion you offered others. And your conscientiousness, the diligence and commitment once exploited to manage someone else's chaos, can now fuel your healing with the same dedication. These Super Traits, when redirected toward yourself rather than manipulators, become the foundation of your recovery rather than tools for your exploitation. That's because the qualities that made you vulnerable were never flaws. They're sacred. They're rare.

If you're just learning that now and you feel discouraged, disoriented, and cracked open, I promise you that what they used to harm you is still yours. And they're exactly what you'll use to rebuild.

FROM TRAUMA

It haunts me how deeply relationships with the Dark Tetrad can devastate those they exploit and how little warning we receive about this form of abuse. That's why I wrote this book. For all of you. To give you the language I never had. To help you recognize what's happening before you lose yourself entirely. To show you that what you're experiencing has a name, a pattern, and a path forward. Because when you can name what happens to women with Super Traits at the hands of the Dark Tetrad, you reclaim your power to understand it, survive it, and eventually, transform it.

I wrote this not just to share my story, but to illuminate yours, and to hand you the map I had to draw for myself in the dark. What happened with Tyler wasn't a misunderstanding. He knew what to escalate, when to withhold, and how to keep me guessing. The gaslighting. The push-pull. The hollow intimacy. The calculated guilt. They're all dark personality tactics intended to bleed a woman's sense of reality dry. However, the chaos I experienced had a blueprint I couldn't see until I was already trapped inside it. But it wasn't until months after I finally emerged that I recognized the deeper pattern: Dark Tetrads seek what they lack.

That's because Dark Tetrads feed off what they cannot generate. My empathy filled their void of callousness. My loyalty covered their opportunism. My conscientiousness offset their recklessness. In a sense, we were mirror images. Where I carried depth, they carried emptiness; where I offered stability, they offered manipulation. Research confirms it: They are profoundly deficient in the very Super Traits they target. And they slip past your defenses with borrowed charm and counterfeit empathy, installing themselves before you even realize you've been infiltrated.

The scale of this hidden epidemic is staggering. Sandra L Brown studied thousands of survivors, the majority of whom were functional women with exceptional qualities. These weren't women with codependency issues. They were the calm ones in the room. The ones others leaned on. Empathy came naturally to them. Responsibility was their natural rhythm. They held the line when things got hard. They were the safe havens: reliable, steady, and generous with their trust. And that's precisely what made them targets. And what makes us targets. Our instinct to offer acceptance without judgment, to listen without rejection, and to stay when others would leave makes these Super Traits perfect vessels for exploitation by those incapable of generating their own emotional resources.

So, why are these women so often branded as codependent, a label that is not even recognized in the DSM-5 as a psychological disorder? Because much of what looks like low self-worth or dependency is actually cognitive dissonance, a psychological war between what you know and what you're told.

The betrayal trauma commonly experienced with the Dark Tetrad shatters the very Super Traits that serve you brilliantly everywhere else. The emotional intelligence that advances your career, the loyalty that makes you a cherished friend, and the conscientiousness that fuels your achievements all become weapons turned against you.

And it rewires you. Your nervous system learns to live in confusion with all the cortisol, the dissociation, and the constant hypervigilance. Kindness becomes suspect. Safety feels temporary. All of this then makes friendship, work relationships, and family connections feel precarious. You then move through life braced for betrayal. Eventually, when you consider dating again, the prospect alone can trigger panic. That's because the traumatic memory is stored in the body even if the source is gone.

A recent study confirmed what I was living. Among intimate partners of individuals with psychopathic traits, 83% showed symptoms of PTSD, a rate higher than survivors of physical violence. More than half had moderate to severe depression. Nearly all reported emotional abuse. 98%. And most endured four or five forms of harm at once: sexual, financial, psychological, and emotional. The marks Brian left on my skin healed. Tyler never raised a hand, but he didn't have to, as the damage lived in my gut, my jaw, my heartbeat, and in my sleep. It embedded itself in my biology.

And beneath all that physical and psychological tension lurked something even more insidious: shame. Shame that burrows deeper than any bruise could reach. The numbers tell a devastating story: 87% of betrayal survivors shouldered blame that never belonged to them. We spiral into shame, question our judgment, and replay every red flag we missed. When I finally went to therapy, the first few therapists wanted to talk about my childhood and my attachment style. They saw my devastation and labeled it codependency, as if my loyalty was the pathology, not Tyler's exploitation of it. Their well-meaning but ill-informed approach only compounded my shame: now I wasn't just betrayed, I was broken.

Sandra L. Brown's research was the first thing that made sense of how I could fall into the trap again and again. I didn't stay because I was weak. I stayed because I was loyal. I didn't fall apart because I was codependent. I fell apart because I was betrayed. My withdrawal, self-blame, and emotional collapse were the natural aftermath of betrayal trauma, the normal response of a healthy nervous system to calculated harm.

I wrote this book so you can forgive your supposed naivety and see it for what it is: a capacity for depth. To replace self-blame with fierce self-compassion. To show you how to protect the very qualities that made you a target, because these same strengths, properly guarded, will lead you back to yourself.

Here's the truth that will set you free: You were never the broken one. You were the extraordinary one. Your depth of feeling, your capacity to commit, and your willingness to see the best in others aren't flaws. They're your superpowers. But now, you're going to have to channel that same incredible strength inward to heal. You'll have to fight for yourself harder than you ever fought for him. Some days, you won't feel like it. You'll want to disappear. Numb out. Slide backward. Bargain with the past.

But the darker the path, the more you need to believe in the light you've always carried. Your strengths were distorted but not erased. Borrowed but not stolen. And now, they're waiting to be reclaimed and transformed into something even more powerful than before.

This is where you stop selling yourself short. This is where you burn the script he handed you and write your own ending.

TO RESILIENCY

Maybe you've gotten out. Or maybe your Brian or Tyler still lives under your roof. You've continued to give them one more chance, but something in you knows they will not change. That's because Dark Tetrad individuals seldom do. Your attempts at healing together will keep getting sabotaged by a man fundamentally unequipped to care in the way you need, and this changes everything. It's the moment you stop trying to make sense of the abuser and start choosing yourself again and again.

But the bad news bears repeating: It's going to be messy, especially early on. Even if you're doing well on the surface, there are emotional, physical, neurological layers that take time to unravel. You placed your safety in the hands of a person who used your nervous system like a resource, twisted your instincts for their gain, and rewrote your reality in slow, deliberate strokes.

So, you'll sometimes spiral. Wake up at 3 a.m. in panic. Rehash every red flag. Rage at your loyalty. Loop through old texts and wonder how you missed it.

That's your brain trying to make sense of a distorted reality. It's searching for patterns. Rebuilding trust with your gut. That process, when done deliberately and with structure, transforms you. And if you're willing to do the work, the chances are high you'll come out stronger than before the wrecking ball hit. Research on post-traumatic growth (PTG) shows that *over half* of trauma survivors come back stronger than before, like a broken bone that heals more densely at the fracture point. And if PTG is possible for the average trauma survivor, women with Super Traits are practically built to crush this recovery journey.

Always remember, your Super Traits aren't the problem. They're the power. The key is approaching your recovery with the same qualities that made you a target. Trust and straightforwardness. Efficiency and dependability. Altruism and loyalty. Self-discipline and deliberateness. These are the same traits that I used to build back stronger, the ones I continue to leverage today.

What they weaponized against you becomes your greatest strength. What they tried to drain becomes your wellspring. It's the plot twist they never saw coming. The phoenix they tried to burn, rising stronger from the very ashes they created. And trust me, there's nothing more spectacular than a woman who's reclaimed her power from someone who thought they'd stolen it for good.

THE PATH FORWARD

There is hope. You can emerge from the trauma stronger, wiser, and a better version of yourself. But PTG won't happen without your consent. It won't always feel good, but the pain will heal you as it emerges through the struggle to make meaning from it. Not from moving on quickly, but from sitting with it. Engaging with it. Naming the patterns. Learning what made you vulnerable and what makes you resilient. Remember: It's not what happened, but what we do next. So struggle well, love yourself fiercely and without compromise, and you *will* come out stronger.

SELF-CARE

Clarity is not just part of PTG. It's the foundation, the framework, and the finish line together. And you can't get clear with a foggy mind or an exhausted body. That's why when I left Tyler, I got honest about what numbed me out and what brought me back. I went all in on sobriety. I stopped cutting corners on my health and prioritized sleep, clean eating, and regular movement. I got honest about what numbed me out and what brought me back.

Research shows that when survivors refuse to face their painful emotions, a pattern called experiential avoidance, they dramatically limit their potential for PTG. In plain English, that means numbing out, denying, or bypassing your emotional pain comes at the cost of long-term growth.

So, leverage that conscientiousness of yours instead. Be loyal to yourself the way you once were to him. Set some non-negotiables of self-care, such as activities that reliably contribute to your well-being. Maybe it's reading or journaling, yoga or hiking. Whatever it is, prescribe it and follow it with the same discipline you once used to maintain a relationship that was killing you.

Your body is trying to tell you things. Your emotions are data points. Let them come through clean, without the static of substances, exhaustion, or neglect. You need a clear transmission now more than ever.

EDUCATION & SELF-FORGIVENESS

Learning about Super Traits saved me. It reframed my story and showed me I wasn't alone. Here I was, successful in my career, financially independent, and respected in my field, yet I was drowning in relationships with one dark personality after another. For most of my adult life, that contrast was jarring. How could I be so competent everywhere else yet so consistently entangled with men who exploited me? Turns out, I wasn't the exception. I was the rule. I wasn't weak; I was strong in all the ways that made me a perfect target. My Super Traits, the very qualities that powered my success elsewhere, were precisely what these men hunted. And finally, that made sense of everything.

So, start reading everything you can get your hands on about Super Traits. Start with Sandra L. Brown's *Women Who Love Psychopaths*. It was the book that kickstarted my healing. Learn the patterns that ensnared you with toxic partners in the first place.

Remember: Your self-esteem may have taken a hit as a result of your relationships, but that doesn't mean you're fundamentally flawed. It means your authenticity met his manipulation, and manipulation won temporarily. Yes, you got played. But you weren't playing a game. You were operating with honesty and integrity in a relationship you thought was real. He, on the other hand, was running a long con. To protect yourself going forward, you don't need to become like him. You just need to recognize the game when you see it and refuse to be the board they play on.

INTENTIONAL REFLECTION

Take time to reflect. The form varies, but the principle remains the same: Growth comes from repeated, deliberate reflection. Ask questions like, *What did I learn?* or *How can I protect myself going forward?* For me, it was journaling. Spilling uncensored, messy truths onto the page every day. For you, it might be songwriting, painting, or voice memos. The medium doesn't matter as much as the presence and expression.

Record what was real, what you felt, what you denied. Track your emotions without self criticism. More than likely, part of what will come up is anger. Raw anger. Hollenbeck and Steffens reported that 84% of women who've experienced betrayal trauma reported anger so intense it felt unfamiliar. So when it arises, pour your rage onto the page. That anger isn't pathology. Rather, it's the seed of self-compassion, your emotional response to perceiving your suffering clearly for the first time. It's the part of you that finally recognizes: This shouldn't have happened, and I deserve better.

From this recognition, ask yourself: *What values did I compromise? What matters most now? What's worth protecting at all costs?* Create a personal manifesto, one page that crystallizes what you believe now about yourself, about love, about safety, and about your worth. Make sure to also use discomfort as a compass. When grief or anger surface, ask, *What sacred value of mine was violated here?*

PROCESS IN COMMUNITY

There will be times when you'll want to isolate and sit with your feelings. That's okay. But don't get stuck there. Research shows that one of the strongest predictors of PTG is meaningful social support. Not surface-level sympathy. Not advice disguised as concern. What matters is connection, the kind that helps you feel seen, heard, and held.

Find a licensed therapist or experienced coach who gets you. I'll be honest, most aren't familiar with Super Traits yet, and that's okay. What matters is finding someone open to learning, who listens without judgment, and who recognizes the strengths beneath your pain. If they pathologize your loyalty as codependency or call your conscientiousness people-pleasing, walk away. You can bring Sandra L. Brown's work into sessions, as many good practitioners are eager to incorporate new frameworks. What you can't compromise on is being treated with dignity. You deserve a space where your trauma is understood, not dissected, dismissed, or just blamed on your childhood.

Speak your truth in safe places. Telling your story out loud helps reintegrate the fragmented pieces of trauma into a coherent, livable narrative. You can journal, share in trauma-informed groups, and talk with a trusted friend. You don't have to say everything. But say something.

And here's the nuance: Social support isn't a magic fix. The same principle applies in public as in private: If you're minimizing your pain, bypassing it, trying to act like you're fine, you'll block the very help that could help you grow. That's because people can only support the truth you're willing to face.

PATTERN RECOGNITION & BOUNDARIES

I saw a talk online where Sandra L. Brown said something like this: "Conscientiousness bit you in the butt because you weren't impulsive enough. You didn't cut and run on the first red flag, or the fiftieth."

She was absolutely right about my Super Traits working against me. My thoroughness, ability to weigh all sides, and resistance to snap judgments kept me invested long after the evidence screamed "Danger!" But what once kept me trapped can now be repurposed for protection.

Start by developing a trust filter. Use that conscientiousness to identify specific behaviors or inconsistencies that will raise red flags in the future. Identify patterns you experienced across partners. Document them. Review them. Apply this filter to every relationship going forward, whether romantic, professional, or platonic.

Practice micro-boundaries in daily life. Say no to small things to rebuild your sense of agency. Your conscientiousness makes you perfectly suited to track people's responses. So, track if they respect your no, or if they push back. This methodical approach sharpens the intuition that was dulled by gaslighting.

Keep a gut log. Any time your body says no but you override it, write it down. That same detail-oriented nature that helped you organize your ex's chaos can now help you track when and why you abandon yourself. Over time, this helps you realign with your knowing.

The same traits that made you stay loyal to the wrong person can become the traits that help you defend your boundaries now. Turn that conscientiousness toward protecting yourself instead of accommodating them.

REDISCOVER PURPOSE

One of the hallmarks of PTG is opening to new possibilities, including career shifts, new goals, and creative expression. For me, I am allowing more space for writing, speaking, and teaching, becoming the advocate I wish I'd had. I've reclaimed my love of painting, a passion I lost somewhere along my checkered romantic past.

What did you love before him? Before all of them? What lights you up that got dimmed in their chaos? That part of you that finishes what it starts, honors your word, and keeps showing up can now be directed toward goals that serve you. The very trait that kept you tethered to chaos can be transformed into your anchor to stability.

Let me offer one empathetic caution here. That conscientiousness in you might be screaming for a plan, a timeline, and measurable progress to push for closure, for efficiency, for some kind of finish line you can cross and be done with the mess. It wants to fix everything, and fix it now. This is where your agreeableness, particularly your capacity for empathy and tolerance, needs to balance things out. Extend that same patience and understanding to yourself that you so readily give to others. Your healing doesn't need to be efficient; it needs to be thorough. Your pain doesn't need a solution; it needs compassion.

By all means, be responsible about your healing. Be determined. Set those therapy appointments. Journal regularly. But don't let that conscientiousness become a taskmaster that rushes what can't be rushed. Know when it's time to set down the planner and just be present with whatever surfaces.

Permit yourself to heal at your own pace. Don't expect a clean arc. Let healing be what it is: nonlinear, slow, and sacred. Sometimes you'll backslide. Sometimes you'll rage. Sometimes you'll feel nothing at all. And all of it is exactly where you need to be.

Your Super Traits are perfectly designed to help you through this, but only when they work together, not against each other. Trust the process. Trust yourself. It takes time. But you're equipped for this in ways you don't even realize yet.

THE WOMAN YOU BECOME

You walk into a room, and for the first time in forever, you're not scanning for danger. You're present with curiosity, with your shoulders back and breath steady.

The stranger across from you says something slightly off-color. Your body tenses and braces for the familiar spiral. But instead, you simply think: *That didn't land right with me.* No panic. No mental gymnastics.

Clarity.

This future isn't some fairytale place where you magically forget everything that happened. No, this is real life, where occasionally the smell of a certain cologne or the cadence of someone's laugh can still throw you back into the fog. But now? You know how to pull yourself out. You recognize when your nervous system is sending outdated alerts. You feel the trigger, you recognize it, and you move through with your composure intact.

Remember the first time you heard yourself apologize for something he did? Now picture yourself sitting with a friend, telling her about someone you've been seeing. "He's charming and successful, but every time I voice an opinion, he dismisses it. I've realized he's not for me," you say, your voice steady. No shame, no scrambling to explain. Just the calm certainty of someone who refuses to shrink for someone else's comfort.

Now see yourself standing barefoot on the new floors you chose, surrounded by paint colors no one questioned or criticized. You start multiple projects and finish them at your own pace. When you handle finances, you don't question your competence. Your decisions belong to you again. The mental committee of critics has been fired.

The ex who burned your world down texts at 2 a.m., wanting closure or sex or validation or whatever they're calling to fix their need for supply this week. You don't respond, and the world doesn't end. Your compassion remains intact, but now you direct it toward yourself first.

When a well-meaning mother asks why you're "still single," you smile and say, "I'm enjoying my life and open to someone who adds to it, not completes it." No defensive tone, no hidden shame. You know your worth isn't measured by relationship status because you're the prize, not the contestant.

You sit across from someone new. Maybe it's been months since you last tried this, maybe years. But something's different. You're not rushing to impress, to secure their approval, to lock in validation. You're curious. You ask questions and listen to the answers instead of preparing your response. You notice their body language, how they treat the server, and whether they ask you anything about yourself. If the connection grows, it grows. If it fades, you let it. You've learned that the loss of an illusion is no loss at all. Your Super Traits now serve as protection rather than points of exploitation.

This is the quiet revolution your past partners never anticipated. While they remain trapped in their cycles, you've reclaimed your power. The trust and devotion they once twisted against you now stand as your guardians. These qualities, evolved and fortified by self-respect, are now untouchable by strategies that once slipped so easily past your defenses.

You remember every moment in vivid detail now. Your Super Traits ensured you felt it all, noticed everything, and remained awake through the nightmare. You stayed present. You faced the pain with open eyes. And that unwavering attentiveness, that boundless compassion you once lavished on someone incapable of comprehending its worth? That's your crown now. You carried the pain and transmuted it into strength and grace. And you survived because you discovered who you've been all along.

I'd love to tell you this transformation happens overnight. That you'll awake one morning completely healed, magically immune to manipulation, and fully recovered from the deep wound of betrayal. But the truth is messier, slower, and more cyclical. Some mornings, you'll still awaken with their voice in your head. Some nights, you'll still wonder what is wrong with you that you didn't see it sooner. You'll imagine their seemingly carefree life and feel a flash of anger at the unfairness. You'll cry sometimes. You'll still get triggered.

But these moments grow farther apart. And now you know how to hold it. You meet your pain with compassion. You speak to yourself gently. You stop the spiral, and you come back home. Your peace belongs to you now, something they can neither touch nor understand. The difference isn't that you never stumble. It's that you know how to get back up without tearing yourself apart in the process. You know your strength was forged in fire.

When you first leave a Dark Tetrad relationship, survival consumes everything. Your nervous system screams danger. Your finances hemorrhage. Your mind loops through trauma like a broken record. Getting through each day demands every ounce of strength. But here's the plot twist in your story: What was meant to destroy you becomes the foundation you rebuild upon. What they used to harm you transforms into your greatest protection. The very traits they exploited become your most powerful allies, not in spite of what happened, but because of how you fought your way back.

Wherever you find yourself, know: This is the beginning.

The woman you become after surviving someone from the Dark Tetrad doesn't just recover what was lost. She discovers what was waiting to be born.

REAL TALK: GUARD YOUR GLOW

You've made it to the end. But this isn't closure. This is the initiation.

If you've been reading with a lump in your throat, if the dots have connected and something in you feels freshly awake, don't rush past it. Hold space for this moment.

I spent years thriving in most areas of my life, with a successful career, solid friendships, and community respect, even as my love life crumbled under the weight of men who targeted exactly what made me exceptional. It took Sandra L. Brown's research and my fight for survival to finally see the pattern. What I once saw as my weakness turned out to be my greatest strength. I was able to recalibrate and rebuild trust in myself. And you can too!

Over time, you'll catch the patterns. Your body will warn you when someone takes more than they deserve. You'll recognize when you're overriding your boundaries to maintain harmony or fulfill others' expectations. And you'll adjust faster each time.

This is how your new life gets built: through one honest check-in at a time. The journey never ends, but your strength and discernment grows with every conscious choice. What made you vulnerable is now your greatest source of power and your focus will be directed toward people who are worthy of your glow.

You're not who you were when you picked up this book. And you're not going back.

Your Super Traits are the roots of who you are. You were wired to glow.

📖 Journal Coaching Moment

This final practice is simple. It's your first act of living differently, and identifying what's sacred.

- Write down your top three Super Traits. Whatever feels most like you.

- Reflect on the times your Super Traits have shown up to protect or guide you.

- Consider how honoring your Super Traits can shape your boundaries and choices going forward.

- What's one small step you can take today to live more fully aligned with these core parts of yourself?

If you need help identifying them, here's a breakdown of the traits:

Agreeableness

- *Trust:* You assume the best. You see others through who you are.

- *Straightforwardness:* You're honest and open. You speak the truth.

- *Altruism:* You care deeply. You compromise naturally.

- *Cooperation:* You work toward harmony, not because you're weak, but because peace matters to you.

- *Modesty:* You're grounded and self-effacing. The opposite of narcissism.

- *Empathy:* You feel with people. Tender-minded and kind, even when it hurts.

- *Loyalty:* You stay. Sometimes too long. But when you commit, you mean it.

- *Tolerance:* You give space. You hold room, even when it costs you.

Conscientiousness

- *Efficiency:* You step up. You make it work. You make stuff happen.

- *Organization:* You bring order to chaos.

- *Dependability:* You follow through. You're the one people count on.

- *Achievement Orientation:* You aim high. And you hustle hard.

- *Self-Discipline:* When others bail, you control your urges and stay focused.

- *Deliberateness:* You're careful. You weigh things. You stick to what you believe.

Conclusion:
Guard Your Glow

Three years ago, I sat in my therapist's office, asking the same question that brought you to *Wired to Glow*: "How could this happen to me again?"

I had experience. I had the education. I'd spent years reading about attachment styles, trauma bonds, and codependency. I understood terms like people-pleasing and love addiction. I'd absorbed the common advice: Heal your inner child, raise your standards, stop chasing, and raise your vibration. I knew the language. I tried some and knew enough not to waste my time with others.

But nothing explained why I kept losing myself in relationships that looked like love in the beginning and left me hollow.

In one of those sessions, my coach introduced me to Sandra L. Brown's research on relational harm and Super Traits. That's when the shame started to dissipate. For the first time, things make sense. It wasn't a matter of unhealed wounds or subconscious sabotage. Agreeableness and conscientiousness made me resilient in life but exposed in love. Everything changed once I understood how these personality traits were used against me. And although that shift didn't erase the damage, it did give me a foundation. And from there, I began to rebuild.

I wrote this book from my home in Chattanooga, a space I chose, decorated according to my tastes, and filled it with evidence of the life I've built from the ground up. My dog Sakara sleeps at my feet. My art supplies are scattered across the table where I've been rediscovering the creativity that got buried under years of chaos. The walls display paintings I never had time to create when I was managing someone else's moods. The bookshelves hold volumes I'm actually reading instead of just buying and hoping to get to someday. My calendar includes hiking trips, art classes, dinners with friends who have never had to wonder if I'm okay. People who know the real me and celebrate me.

My work has evolved, too. What started as corporate behavioral health has expanded into writing, speaking, and coaching women through their recognition journeys. The same traits that left me exposed now fuel meaningful work that protects other women from walking the path I walked.

Now, when I encounter manipulation in business, in social settings, and in those inevitable moments when someone tests my boundaries, I recognize it immediately. My nervous system still responds, but now it's information rather than confusion. The hypervigilance has transformed into discernment. This is PTG in living color, proof that you can become not just who you were before, but someone stronger, wiser, and more authentically yourself than you ever imagined possible.

Since I began writing this book, the conversation around pathological relationships has exploded. Narcissistic abuse and trauma bonding have entered mainstream vocabulary. True crime documentaries dissect high-profile cases of manipulation and control. And videos go viral with stories that look a lot like ours. This visibility is progress, but it's also created new problems. The term "narcissist" gets thrown around so casually now that it's lost its clinical meaning. Kindhearted friends even diagnose exes based on social media clips. Overall, the complex pattern of exploitation, grooming, and erosion that defines pathological relationships gets watered down.

What's still missing is education. Real, research-backed education about why women with Super Traits are often the ones targeted, why we don't leave when relationships go toxic, and why the damage cuts so deep. The Institute for Relational Harm Reduction & Public Pathology Education continues to expand this work. More therapists are learning to recognize relational harm as a category of trauma. But not fast enough. Survivors are still being misdiagnosed and told that we were codependent, enmeshed, or simply stuck. But we don't have time to wait for the field to catch up. We need tools *now*. We need each other *now*.

My story is far from rare. That's what's heartbreaking. And unless we interrupt the pattern, it will keep happening to the next generation of women.

I think about the young women in my family, brilliant, compassionate, and driven. I see their Super Traits developing, their natural tendency to trust, invest, and see the best in others. And I know that somewhere out there, men are learning to spot and exploit those exact qualities.

But here's what gives me hope: Every woman who learns to guard her glow becomes a beacon for others. Every time you trust your instincts instead of overriding them, you model healthy boundaries. Every time you refuse to explain away red flags, you give another woman permission to do the same.

This goes beyond personal healing. It's generational change.

For women with Super Traits, the challenges will likely continue beyond romantic relationships. Dark Tetrad men rise quickly in high-stakes industries such as finance, tech, law, medicine, and politics because their traits aren't seen as dysfunction in those contexts. Rather, they're seen as powerful, strategic, unflinching, and sometimes even visionary. Narcissists get promoted for their confidence. Machiavellians advance through ruthlessness. Psychopaths are admired for their risk tolerance. Sadists find cover in cutthroat environments where domination gets conflated with leadership.

And your Super Traits, the same qualities that made you exceptional at everything except recognizing romantic red flags, will face similar exploitation in boardrooms, on teams, and in negotiations. The patterns repeat, just with different costumes. Love bombing masquerades as mentorship. Gaslighting hides behind the language of constructive feedback. Isolation shows up as exclusion from key decisions. Financial control gets repackaged as budget manipulation or delayed promotions.

Learning to guard your glow in love is just the beginning. The real work is carrying that protection into every area of your life to safeguard your Super Traits to ensure they cannot be weaponized.

You don't need to become harder. You need to become more yourself, with sharper tools, stronger boundaries, and a clearer sense of what you will and will not allow.

••

This book is ending, but your story is just beginning. You have everything you need to build a life that honors your worth, protects your gifts, and refuses to settle for anything less than you deserve.

Toxic men aren't the headline here. The real story is the life you're building, one rooted in your values, protected by your Super Traits, and filled with connection, clarity, and purpose. That's what makes you magnetic to the right people and untouchable to the wrong ones.

Your Super Traits are not accidents. Nor are they burdens. And despite what you've been through, they aren't liabilities. They're your superpowers, meant to support your life and enrich the connections you *freely choose.*

This is where the shift happens:

- You listen to your body and honor what it tells you.

- You enforce boundaries without performing an apology.

- You study the tactics so you're never caught off guard again.

- You take up space in rooms where you used to dim your light.

- You build a community that reflects your worth to you.

- You tell your story on your terms and when you're ready.

This transformation doesn't happen all at once. It builds on the small, gritty everyday choices you make. Every time you say no, every time you walk away, and every time you stop trying to earn love that should've been given freely.

The woman I am today doesn't miss him. I grieve the energy I spent contorting myself to win someone who never deserved it. That version of me is gone. And in her place is someone steady, clear, and loyal to herself.

Your glow was never the problem.

It's always been the solution.

Now go live like you know it.

Acknowledgments

I want to express my deepest gratitude to the people who have shaped me, supported me, and lifted me up when I needed it most.

First, to my late mother, the epitome of Super Traits. She embodied pure, unconditional love, a love so fierce and unwavering that it became the foundation of the woman I am today. Her strength, tenderness, and integrity continue to guide me every day. Everything good in me began with her.

To my soul sister, thank you for being a constant source of light, laughter, and truth. Your presence in my life has been both grounding and inspiring, and I'm endlessly grateful for the bond we share and for being my spiritual north star through it all.

To BB, my ride or die—your loyalty, friendship, and love mean more to me than I can say. You've reminded me not to hide my talent "under a bushel" and to stop downplaying what I bring to the world. Your perspective challenges me in the best way.

To Kristy, you've been one of the most steady, loyal, and non-judgmental friends I've ever known. You're adventurous, brilliant, an incredible mom, and truly one of a kind. I'm so lucky to call you my friend.

To the OG, our story has taken many forms throughout the years, but one thing hasn't changed: you're still the funniest boy I know.

To my dad, you didn't have to raise me, but you chose to. And in doing so, you showed me what a good man looks like: steady, kind, consistent, and full of heart.

To Zach, my book coach, thank you for holding space for my story. Your guidance and belief in this message helped bring it to life.

To Deborah, my personal coach, thank you for walking beside me on this wild journey of learning and healing. You introduced me to Sandra L. Brown's work, and through that lens, my entire life began to make sense.

To Sandra L. Brown and the pioneers who dared to speak when few understood, thank you for creating a path forward. And to the mental health professionals who show up daily with courage and compassion, you are the quiet heroes helping others heal. The world is better because of you.

To those who I felt abused my trust—you've been exposed. Your darkness is no longer hidden. You didn't break me—you awakened something stronger. I own my truth, my voice, and my light and I'm not alone. I found my power in myself, in God, and in a community of survivors that refuses to be silenced.

Resources

If you or someone you know is in crisis, struggling with abuse, or seeking help for relationship trauma, the following organizations provide support, education, and intervention services.

CRISIS AND SUICIDE PREVENTION HOTLINES

- 988 Suicide and Crisis Lifeline (United States)
  Call or text 988 to reach trained counselors. Available 24 hours a day, 7 days a week. Webchat available at 988lifeline.org.

- Crisis Text Line
  Text HOME to 741741 for free, confidential support via text message, 24/7.

- International Crisis Lines
  For resources outside the United States, visit findahelpline.com to find crisis hotlines by country.

DOMESTIC VIOLENCE AND ABUSE SUPPORT

- National Domestic Violence Hotline (United States) Call 1-800-799-SAFE (7233) or text START to 88788. Chat available at thehotline.org. Services include crisis intervention, safety planning, and referrals to shelters and legal aid.

NARCISSISTIC ABUSE AND RELATIONSHIP TRAUMA RESOURCES

- Institute for Relational Harm Reduction & Public Pathology Education
Founded by Sandra L. Brown, M.A., this organization provides education and tools for recovery from pathological love relationships. Visit saferelationshipsmagazine.com and womenwholovepsychopaths.com.

- The Association for NPD & Psychopathy Survivors (ANPPS)
Offers resources for understanding narcissistic personality disorder, psychopathy, and finding specialized support. Visit anpps.org.

These resources are a starting point for safety, healing, and education.

References

CHAPTER ONE

1. Sandra L. Brown, *Women Who Love Psychopaths: Inside the Relationships of Inevitable Harm With Psychopaths, Sociopaths & Narcissists*, 3rd ed. (Oak Island, NC: The Institute for Relational Harm Reduction & Public Pathology Education, 2018).

2. Nicholas S. Holtzman and Michael J. Strube, "People with Dark Personalities Tend to Create a Physically Attractive Veneer," *Social Psychological and Personality Science* 4, no. 4 (2013): 461–467.

3. Jauk, Emanuel, Aljoscha C. Neubauer, Thomas Mairunteregger, Stephanie Pemp, Katharina P. Sieber, and Tyler F. Rauthmann. "How alluring are dark personalities? The dark triad and attractiveness in speed dating." *European Journal of Personality* 30, no. 2 (2016): 125–138.

4. Furnham, Adrian, Steven C. Richards, and Delroy L. Paulhus. "The Dark Triad of Personality: A 10 year review." *Social and Personality Psychology Compass* 7, no. 3 (2013): 199-216.

5. Juliana G. Breines and Serena Chen, "Self-Compassion Increases Self-Improvement Motivation," *Personality and Social Psychology Bulletin* 38, no. 9 (2012): 1133–1143.

CHAPTER TWO

1. Holly M. Baughman, Peter K. Jonason, Minna Lyons, and Philip A. Vernon, "Liar Liar Pants on Fire: Cheater Strategies Linked to the Dark Triad," *Personality and Individual Differences* 71 (2014): 35–38.

2. Emanuel Jauk and Raoul Dieterich, "Addiction and the Dark Triad of Personality," *Frontiers in Psychiatry* 10 (2019): 662.

3. Irena Boskovic, Luciano Giromini, Ali Yunus Emre Akca, Cristina Mazza, and Paolo Roma, "Faking Bad, Faking Good and the Dark Tetrad: Relationship Between Spontaneous Faking, History of Faking Behaviour, Propensity to Fake and Dark Tetrad," *International Journal of Forensic Mental Health* (2025): 14999013251326582.

CHAPTER THREE

1. Zou, Zhiling, Hongwen Song, Yuting Zhang, and Xiaochu Zhang. "Romantic Love vs. Drug Addiction May Inspire a New Treatment for Addiction: *Frontiers in Psychology* 7 (2016): 187913.

2. Smith, Martin J. *Understanding and Dealing with Controlling, Intimidating and Manipulative Personalities.* Springer Nature Switzerland, 2024.

3. Brazil, Kristopher J., and Adelle E. Forth. "Psychopathy and the Induction of Desire: Formulating and Testing an Evolutionary Hypothesis." *Evolutionary Psychological Science* 6, no. 1 (2020): 64–81.

CHAPTER FOUR

1. Strutzenberg, Claire. "Love-Bombing: A Narcissistic Approach to Relationship Formation." (2016).

2. Brazil, Kristopher J., Chantelle J. Dias, and Adelle E. Forth. "Successful and Selective Exploitation in Psychopathy: Convincing others and gaining trust." *Personality and Individual Differences* 170 (2021): 110394.

3. Nitschinsk, Lewis, Stephanie J. Tobin, and Eric J. Vanman. "The Dark Triad and Online Self-Presentation Styles and Beliefs." *Personality and Individual Differences* 194 (2022): 111641.

4. Robinson, Joanna. "What Is NXIVM, the Sex Cult Explored in The Vow?" *Esquire*, August 23, 2020. https://www.esquire.com/entertainment/tv/a33658764/what-is-nxivm-sex-cult-celebrities-stars-the-vow-hbo-true-story/.

5. Durvasula, Ramani S. *It's Not You: Identifying and Healing from Narcissistic People.* New York: BenBella Books, 2024.

CHAPTER FIVE

1. Zana Babakr and Nabi Fatahi, "Risk-Taking Behaviour: The Role of Dark Triad Traits, Impulsivity, Sensation Seeking and Adverse Childhood Experience," *Acta Informatica Medica* 31, no. 4 (2023): 292.

2. Emanuel Jauk and Raoul Dieterich, "Addiction and the Dark Triad of Personality," *Frontiers in Psychiatry* 10 (2019): 662.

3. Stephen M. Doerfler, Maryam Tajmirriyahi, William Ickes, and Peter K. Jonason, "The Self-Concepts of People with Dark Triad Traits Tend to Be Weaker, Less Clearly Defined, and More State-Related," *Personality and Individual Differences* 180 (2021): 110977.

CHAPTER SIX

1. Hare, Robert D. "This Charming Psychopath." *Psychology Today*, January 1, 1994. https://www.psychologytoday.com/us/articles/199401/this-charming-psychopath.

2. Hart, William, Gregory K. Tortoriello, Kyle Richardson, and Christopher J. Breeden. "Profiles and profile comparisons between Dark Triad constructs on self-presentation tactic usage and tactic beliefs." *Journal of Personality* 87, no. 3 (2019): 501-517.

3. Forsyth, Loch, Jeromy Anglim, Evita March, and Barbara Bilobrk. "Dark Tetrad Personality Traits and the Propensity to Lie Across Multiple Contexts." *Personality and Individual Differences* 177 (2021): 110792.

CHAPTER SEVEN

1. Bruce Y. Lee, "How Future Faking Can Be Used to Manipulate You," *Psychology Today*, July 2, 2024, https://www.psychologytoday.com/us/blog/a-funny-bone-to-pick/202406/how-future-faking-can-be-used-to-manipulate-you.

2. Rosemary Parkinson, Stephanie T. Jong, and Sarah Hanson, "Subtle or Covert Abuse Within Intimate Partner Relationships: A Scoping Review," *Trauma, Violence, & Abuse* 25, no. 5 (2024): 4,090–4,101.

3. Sarah Halpern-Meekin, Wendy D. Manning, Peggy C. Giordano, and Monica A. Longmore, "Relationship Churning, Physical Violence, and Verbal Abuse in Young Adult Relationships," *Journal of Marriage and Family* 75, no. 1 (2013): 2–12.

4. Dmitriy S. Kornienko, Milena V. Baleva, and Nadezhda P. Yachmeneva, "Materialism, the Dark Triad Traits, and Money Management Among Undergraduate Students," *Psychology in Russia: State of the Art* 17, no. 2 (2024): 50–63.

5. Monika Prusik and Michał Szulawski, "The Relationship Between the Dark Triad Personality Traits, Motivation at Work, and Burnout Among HR Recruitment Workers," *Frontiers in Psychology* 10 (2019): 1290.

6. Neff, Kristin D, "Self-compassion, Self-esteem, and Well-Being." *Social and Personality Psychology Compass* 5, no. 1 (2011): 1-12.

CHAPTER EIGHT

1. Integrative Life Center, "Effects of Betrayal on the Brain: How to Heal Your Mind and Body," May 3, 2024, https://integrativelifecenter.com/intimacy-disorders/effects-of-betrayal-on-the-brain-how-to-heal-your-mind-and-body/.

2. Jennifer J. Freyd, "Betrayal Trauma," in *Encyclopedia of Psychological Trauma*, ed. Gilbert Reyes, Jon D. Elhai, and Julian D. Ford (Hoboken, NJ: Wiley, 2008), 76.

3. Samantha Joel, Geoff MacDonald, and Elizabeth Page-Gould, "Wanting to Stay and Wanting to Go: Unpacking the Content and Structure of Relationship Stay/Leave Decision Processes," *Social Psychological and Personality Science* 9, no. 6 (2018): 631–44.

4. Bessel van der Kolk, *The Body Keeps the Score: Brain, Mind, and Body in the Healing of Trauma* (New York: Viking, 2014).

5. Robyn L. Gobin, "Partner Preferences among Survivors of Betrayal Trauma," *Journal of Trauma & Dissociation* 13, no. 2 (2012): 152–74.

CHAPTER NINE

1. Nathan W. Hudson, "Lighten the Darkness: Personality Interventions Targeting Agreeableness Also Reduce Participants' Levels of the Dark Triad," *Journal of Personality* 91, no. 4 (2023): 901–16.

2. Stephen M. Doerfler, Maryam Tajmirriyahi, William Ickes, and Peter K. Jonason, "The Self-Concepts of People with Dark Triad Traits Tend to Be Weaker, Less Clearly Defined, and More State-Related," *Personality and Individual Differences* 180 (2021): 110977, https://doi.org/10.1016/j.paid.2021.110977.

3. Omar Minwalla, *The Secret Sexual Basement* (2021), accessed June 13, 2025, https://www.pattyklochko.com/wp-content/uploads/2021/12/The-Secret-Sexual-Basement_7_6_21.pdf.

4. Paul L. Hokemeyer, *Fragile Power: Why Having Everything Is Never Enough* (Center Street, 2019).

5. Delroy L. Paulhus and Patrick Klaiber, "HEXACO, Dark Personalities, and Brunswik Symmetry," *European Journal of Personality 34*, no. 4 (2020): 541–42.

CHAPTER TEN

1. Shahida Arabi, "Narcissistic and Psychopathic Traits in Romantic Partners Predict Post-Traumatic Stress Disorder Symptomology: Evidence for Unique Impact in a Large Sample," *Personality and Individual Differences 201* (2023): 111942.

2. Adelle Forth, Sage Sezlik, Seung Lee, Mary Ritchie, Tyler Logan, and Holly Ellingwood, "Toxic Relationships: The Experiences and Effects of Psychopathy in Romantic Relationships," *International Journal of Offender Therapy and Comparative Criminology* 66, no. 15 (2022): 1627–58.

3. Tedeschi and Lawrence G. Calhoun, "Posttraumatic Growth: Conceptual Foundations and Empirical Evidence," *Psychological Inquiry 15*, no. 1 (2004): 1–18.

4. Wu, Xiaoli, Atipatsa C. Kaminga, Wenjie Dai, Jing Deng, Zhipeng Wang, Xiongfeng Pan, and Aizhong Liu. "The prevalence of moderate-to-high posttraumatic growth: A systematic review and meta-analysis." *Journal of Affective Disorders 243* (2019): 408-415.

5. Henson, Charlotte, Didier Truchot, and Amy Canevello. "What promotes post traumatic growth? A systematic review." *European Journal of Trauma & Dissociation 5*, no. 4 (2021): 100195.

6.   Sager, Julia C. "Self-Compassion and Experiential Avoidance: Potential Pathways to Posttraumatic Growth." PhD diss., University of Missouri-Saint Louis, 2023.

7.   Ed. D. Hollenbeck, LMHC, Crystal M., and Barbara Steffens, Ph.D., "Betrayal Trauma Anger: Clinical Implications for Therapeutic Treatment Based on the Sexually Betrayed Partner's Experience Related to Anger After Intimate Betrayal," *Journal of Sex & Marital Therapy 50*, no. 4 (2024): 456–67.